## ABOUT THE EDITOR

BILLY COLLINS is the author of eleven
collections of poetry and the editor of *Poetry
180: A Turning Back to Poetry, 180 More:
Extraordinary Poems for Every Day*, and *Bright
Wings: An Illustrated Anthology of Poems About
Birds*. He was Poet Laureate of the United
States from 2001 to 2003 and New York State
Poet from 2004 to 2006. A former Distin-
guished Professor at Lehman College (City
University of New York), he is a
Distinguished Fellow of the Rollins Winter
Park Institute and a member of the
American Academy of Arts and Letters.

*poetry* 180

*Random House Trade Paperbacks  New York*

*poetry* 180

A TURNING BACK TO POETRY

*Selected and with an Introduction by*

Billy Collins

A RANDOM HOUSE TRADE PAPERBACK ORIGINAL

*Copyright © 2003 by Billy Collins*

All rights reserved under International and
Pan-American Copyright Conventions. Published in the
United States by Random House Trade Paperbacks,
an imprint of The Random House Publishing Group,
a division of Random House, Inc., New York, and
simultaneously in Canada by Random House of
Canada Limited, Toronto.

RANDOM HOUSE TRADE PAPERBACKS and colophon
are registered trademarks of Random House, Inc.

Owing to limitations of space, permission acknowledgments
begin on page 313.

LIBRARY OF CONGRESS CATALOGING-IN-PUBLICATION DATA
Poetry 180: a turning back to poetry/ selected and
with an introduction by Billy Collins.
p.     cm.
Includes index.
ISBN 0-8129-6887-5
1. American poetry—21st century.    I. Title: Poetry One
hundred eighty.    II. Collins, Billy.
PS615 .P6245 2003
811'.608—dc21          2002036949

Random House website address: www.atrandom.com

Printed in the United States of America

29 28 27 26 25 24 23 22

*Book design by Barbara M. Bachman*

# contents

# *poetry* 180: AN INTRODUCTION

*Billy Collins*

A FEW YEARS AGO I FOUND MYSELF ON A CIRCUIT OF readings, traveling around the Midwest from podium to podium. One stop was at an enormous high school south of Chicago. Despite its daunting size—picture a row of lockers receding into infinity—the school holds a "Poetry Day" every year featuring an exuberant range of activities, including poems set to music by students and performed by the high school chorus and a ninety-piece orchestra. As featured poet that year, I found myself caught up in the high spirits of the day, which seemed to be coming directly from the students themselves, rather than being faculty-imposed. After reading to a crowded auditorium, I was approached by a student who presented me with a copy of the school newspaper containing an article she had written about poetry. In that article, I found a memorable summary of the discomfort so many people seem to experience with poetry. "Whenever I read a modern poem," this teenage girl wrote, "it's like my brother has his foot on the back of my neck in the swimming pool."

Poetry 180 was inspired by the desire to remove poetry far from such scenes of torment. The idea behind this printed collection, which is a version of the Library of Congress "180" website, was to assemble a generous selection of short, clear, contemporary poems which any listener could basically "get" on first hearing—poems whose injection of pleasure is immediate. The original website, which continues to be up and running strong, www.loc.gov/poetry/180, is part of a national initiative I developed shortly after being appointed United States Poet Laureate in 2001. The program is called "Poetry 180: A Poem a Day for American High Schools." In creating it, I had hoped the program would suggest to young people the notion that poetry can be a part of everyday life as well as a subject to be studied in the classroom. On the website, I ask high school teachers and administrators to adopt the program by having a new poem read every day—one for each of the roughly 180 days of the school year—as part of the public announcements. Whether the poems are read over a PA system or at the end of a school assembly, students can hear poetry on a daily basis without feeling any pressure to respond. I wanted teachers to refrain from commenting on the poems or asking students "literary" questions about them. No discussion, no explication, no quiz, no midterm, no seven-page paper—just listen to a poem every morning and off you go to your first class.

I might not have come up with such an ambitious national plan—or any plan at all—were it not for the energetic efforts made by previous laureates to spread the word of poetry far and wide. Prior to the democratizing efforts of Joseph Brodsky, who envisioned poetry being handed out at supermarkets and planted in the bed tables of motel rooms next to the Gideon Bible, the post of poet laureate was centered at the Library of Congress in Washington, specifically in a spacious suite of rooms at the top of the magnificent Jefferson Building, complete with a balcony and, as one visitor put it, a "CNN view" of the Capitol. In those days, the position was called "Consultant in Poetry to the Library of Congress"—admittedly, a mouthful with a businesslike sound. It was the habit of many Consultants to relocate to Washington, go to the office a few days a week, and—I can only imagine—wait for the phone to ring. You never knew when some senator would be curious to know who wrote "Two Tramps in Mud Time." According to Mary Jarrell's memoir, she and Randall took advantage of his tenure in the nation's capital by enjoying cultural offerings such as the Budapest string quartet. Maxine Kumin invited Washington-area schoolchildren to the Poetry Room. Robert Penn Warren wisely devoted one of his terms to the writing of *All the King's Men*. But by the time I took office, the laureateship had evolved into a seat from which resourceful plans for the national dissemination of poetry were being launched. And so Poetry 180 became my contribution.

High school is the focus of my program because all too often it is the place where poetry goes to die. While poetry offers us the possibility of modulating our pace, adolescence is commonly driven by the wish to accelerate, to get from zero to sixty in a heartbeat or in a speed-shop Honda. And despite the sometimes heroic efforts of dedicated teachers, many adolescents find poetry—to use their term of ultimate condemnation—boring. What some students experience when they are made to confront a poem might be summed up in a frustrating syllogism:

I understand English.
This poem is written in English.
I have no idea what this poem is saying.

What is "the misfit witch blocks my quantum path?" a reader might well ask. What's up with "a waveform leaps in my belly"? What's a reader to do in the face of such unyielding obtuseness?

But let us hear from the other side of the room. If there is no room in poetry for difficulty, where is difficulty to go? Just as poetry provides a home for ambiguity, it offers difficulty a place to be dramatized if not solved. "Even in our games," asserts John Ciardi, "we demand difficulty." Which explains why hockey is played on ice and why chess involves more than two warring queens chasing each other around the board. During the heyday of Pound, Eliot, Stevens, and Crane—that Mount Rushmore of modernism—difficulty became a criterion for appraising poetic value. The difficulty of composition was extended to the compass of the reader's experience. Opacity became so closely associated with modernist poetry that readers fled in droves into the waiting arms of novelists, where they could relax in the familiar surroundings of social realism. Of course, the conceptual demands some poems make on their reader can provide an essential pleasure, but this is hardly a recommended starting place for readers interested in reclaiming their connection to poetry. Lacking the experience to distinguish between legitimate difficulty and obscurity for its own sake, some readers give up entirely. Randall Jarrell said that poetry was so difficult to write, why should it be difficult to read. Clarity is the real risk in poetry. To be clear means opening yourself up to judgment. The willfully obscure poem is a hiding place where the poet can elude the reader and thus make appraisal impossible, irrelevant—a bourgeois intrusion upon the poem. Which is why much of the commentary on obscure poetry produces the same kind of headache as the poems themselves.

Of course, the more difficult the poem, the more dependent students are on their teachers. Knotty poems give teachers more to explain; but the classroom emphasis on what a poem means can work effectively to kill the poetry spirit. Too often the hunt for Meaning becomes the only approach; literary devices form a field of barbed wire that students must crawl under to get to "what the poet is trying to say," a regrettable phrase which implies that every poem is a failed act of communication. Explication may dominate the teaching of poetry, but there are other ways to increase a reader's intimacy with a poem. A reader can write the poem out, just as Keats or Frost did, or learn how to say a poem out loud, or even internalize a poem by memorizing it. The problem is that none of these activities requires the presence of a teacher. Ideally, interpretation should be one of the pleasures poetry offers. Unfortunately, too often it overshadows the other pleasures of meter, sound, metaphor, and imaginative travel, to name a few.

———

POETRY 180 WAS ALSO MEANT TO EXPOSE HIGH SCHOOL students to the new voices in contemporary poetry. Even if teachers try to keep up with the poetry of the day, textbooks and anthologies typically lag behind the times. My rough count of one popular introductory text has dead authors beating out living ones at a ratio of nine to one. And oddly enough, many of the poems that are still presented as examples of "modern" poetry—Eliot's "The Love Song of J. Alfred Prufrock" or Williams's "The Red Wheelbarrow"—were written more than seventy-five years ago. With a few exceptions, the poems selected for the Poetry 180 website and this book were chosen with the idea of catching the sounds, rhythms, and attitudes of poetry written much more recently. Some of the poems culled from literary magazines are no more than a year or two old. I ruled out any poem that had become a standard offering in textbooks and anthologies. I wanted also to include voices that were not well known. Quite a few of these poems were written by poets I had not heard of before I started scouting for the poems that would suit the purposes of *Poetry 180*. Assembling this anthology gave me a chance to further the cause of some of my favorite poems and also to discover poets who were new to me. The more I searched for poems, the more I became convinced that regardless of what other kinds of poems will be written in years to come, clear, reader-conscious poems are the ones that will broaden the audience of poetry beyond the precincts of its practitioners.

ADMITTEDLY, SOME OF THESE POEMS WERE SELECTED TO appeal to the interests of high school students. Mark Halliday and Jim Daniels both have poems about cars. Nick

Flynn writes about the suspension of physical laws in cartoons. Edward Hirsch has a poem about basketball, and Louis Jenkins has one on football. There are poems about mothers and sons, fathers and daughters. And poems about teaching and learning. Tom Wayman's hilarious and touching "Did I Miss Anything?" will appeal to anyone who has ever missed a class and then had the temerity to ask the teacher that impertinent question. But this anthology is meant for everyone, even if you somehow managed to avoid high school—that crucible where character is formed and where, as one student pointed out, they even make you read *The Crucible*.

One of the most haunting topics in literary discussion (right up there with the "Death of the Novel") is the disappearance of the audience for poetry. Joyce Carol Oates has pointed out the lamentable fact that the number of poetry readers in this country is about the same as the number of people who write poetry. Based on my confrontations with students who want to write poetry but have no interest in reading it, I would say the poets might slightly outnumber the readers. Such a ratio should be kept in mind whenever we hear people extolling the phenomenon of a "poetry renaissance" in America. Yes, more poetry books are being published, and there are more contests, prizes, slams, open-mike nights, and MFA programs; but a large part of these activities take place within a closed circuit. In recent years, poetry has gained momentum as a cultural force, but much of its energy is expended tracing the same circle it has always moved in, appealing to the same insider audience.

Poetry need not be read by everyone—lots of intense activities have small audiences—but surely this distressing ratio can be changed so that poetry is enjoyed by people who have no professional interest in becoming poets. *Poetry 180* is one of many efforts to change the ratio, to beckon people back to poetry by offering them a variety of poems that might snag their interest. I am convinced that for every nonreader of poetry there is a poem waiting to reconnect them to poetry. If a student hears a poem every day, the odds of he or she encountering the right poem increases dramatically. Ideally, *Poetry 180* was aimed at creating a cognitive dissonance in students who "hate poetry" by exposing them to a poem they find themselves loving irresistibly.

THIS COLLECTION IS NOT AN EXACT TRANSCRIPTION OF the poems on the Poetry 180 website. Putting the poems into book form made it possible to include longer poems as well as poems that came to my attention after the website was put up. The website itself has movable parts; it is a kind of poetry jukebox where the songs can be changed and updated to keep the offerings fresh, especially for schools that want to continue to use the program one semester after another. This book, like all printed books, is fixed, but it includes as many different voices as possible to give a sense of the diverse chorus that is singing the songs of American poetry these days.

Unlike a book of prose fiction, which you read straight through following the rabbit of the plot, there are all sorts of ways to read a collection of poems. You can look up poets you are familiar with, you can flip through the pages looking for a title that grabs you, a shape that invites you in. Or you can read the collection cover to cover, forwards or backwards. But with *Poetry 180*, there is something to be said for starting at the beginning and reading just a poem or two each day. Like pills, for the head and the heart.

FOR MY OWN PART, *POETRY 180* HAS BEEN A PLEASURE and a challenge. Finding the first one hundred poems was fairly easy. I just spun my mental Rolodex of contemporary poems that I liked well enough to remember. Locating the remaining eighty was harder, which might say something about the narrow bounds of my taste or the limited store of smart, clear, contemporary poems. I experienced the privilege of any anthologizer of being in control of the selections and thus being able to express through publication the kind of poetry I favor. With its original focus on high school audiences, *Poetry 180* has a public service ring to it, but it is also, admittedly, a big bouquet of poems that I happen to like. To borrow Fran Liebowitz's musical aesthetics: good poems are poems I like and bad poems are poems I don't like. Putting that egocentric position aside, welcome to *Poetry 180*. Flip through the book and pick a poem, any poem. I know every one is an ace, or at least a face card, because I personally rigged the deck.

*POETRY 180* IS THE WORK OF MANY HANDS WHOSE EFFORTS I would like to acknowledge here. Thanks to the members of the Library of Congress staff who formed the original team that got the program up and running: Prosser Gifford, Jill Brett, and Craig D'Ooge for their encouragement and direction; Michael Hughes for handling the permissions issues along with Sara Anderson and Sheryl Cannady; Rob

Sokol, Glenn Ricci, and Dominique Pickett for forming the team led by John Sayers in charge of designing and maintaining the website; Jennifer Rutland for her invaluable multitasking. Thanks are also due to those who suggested poems: Robert Wrigley, Annie Finch, and Rachel Simon, my assistant, who contributed to all aspects of the project. Thanks to Poets House in New York for the use of their immense library. Thanks to Michele Rosenthal for her diligent editorial suggestions. At Random House, thanks to my editor, Tim Farrell, and also to Ivan Held of the trade paperback program, publicist Alexa Cassanos, and, for her benevolent overseeing, Ann Godoff. Abiding gratitude to my friend Chris Calhoun for his chivalric support and to Diane for more than can be expressed here.

*poetry* 180

# Billy Collins

I ask them to take a poem
and hold it up to the light
like a color slide

or press an ear against its hive.

I say drop a mouse into a poem
and watch him probe his way out,

or walk inside the poem's room
and feel the walls for a light switch.

I want them to waterski
across the surface of a poem
waving at the author's name on the shore.

But all they want to do
is tie the poem to a chair with rope
and torture a confession out of it.

They begin beating it with a hose
to find out what it really means.

# Ted Kooser

First, I would have her be beautiful,
and walking carefully up on my poetry
at the loneliest moment of an afternoon,
her hair still damp at the neck
from washing it. She should be wearing
a raincoat, an old one, dirty
from not having money enough for the cleaners.
She will take out her glasses, and there
in the bookstore, she will thumb
over my poems, then put the book back
up on its shelf. She will say to herself,
"For that kind of money, I can get
my raincoat cleaned." And she will.

## Jan Heller Levi

### NOT BAD, DAD, NOT BAD | 003

I think you are most yourself when you're swimming;
slicing the water with each stroke,
the funny way you breathe, your mouth cocked
as though you're yawning.

You're neither fantastic nor miserable
at getting from here to there.
You wouldn't win any medals, Dad,
but you wouldn't drown.

I think how different everything might have been
had I judged your loving
like I judge your sidestroke, your butterfly,
your Australian crawl.

But I always thought I was drowning
in that icy ocean between us,
I always thought you were moving too slowly to save me,
when you were moving as fast as you can.

# Dorianne Laux

I don't remember how it began.
The singing. Judy at the wheel
in the middle of *Sentimental Journey*.
The side of her face glowing.
Her full lips moving. Beyond her shoulder
the little houses sliding by.
And Geri. Her frizzy hair tumbling
in the wind wing's breeze, fumbling
with the words. All of us singing
as loud as we can. Off key.
Not even a semblance of harmony.
Driving home in a blue Comet singing
*I'll Be Seeing You* and *Love Is a Rose*.
The love songs of war. The war songs
of love. Mixing up verses, eras, words.
Songs from stupid musicals.
Coming in strong on the easy refrains.
Straining our middle aged voices
trying to reach impossible notes,
reconstruct forgotten phrases.
Cole Porter's *Anything Goes*.
Shamelessly la la la-ing
whole sections. Forgetting
the rent, the kids, the men,
the other woman. The sad goodbye.

The whole of childhood. Forgetting
the lost dog, Polio. The grey planes
pregnant with bombs. Fields
of white headstones. All of it gone
as we struggle to remember
the words. One of us picking up
where the others leave off. Intent
on the song. Forgetting our bodies,
their pitiful limbs, their heaviness.
Nothing but three throats
beating back the world—Laurie's
radiation treatments. The scars
on Christina's arms. Kim's brother.
Molly's grandfather. Jane's sister.
Singing to the telephone poles
skimming by. Stoplights
blooming green. The road,
a glassy black river edged
with brilliant gilded weeds. The car
an immense boat cutting the air
into blue angelic plumes. Singing
*Blue Moon* and *Paper Moon*
and *Mack the Knife,* and *Nobody Knows
the Trouble I've Seen.*

## Mark Halliday

The pink car is in my head.
It rolls calmly and calmly.
Across the carpet in 1957 and in my head.

Why is it pink? The question does not come up.
The pink car is just what it is and glad so.
Pink is its own color, of its own, being that,
calmly along the quiet roads.

(Pink not anything about sex
and not anything about femininity
and not anything about embarrassment or socialism
those meanings are from outside
whereas this pink car is not coming from an idea
it is a way of being its own self.)

The pink car rolls slowly along a pale green lane
till it needs to go fast then it goes very fast
while still quiet. It knows what it is,
it is the pink car!

Along the lanes to be what it is
it goes around hard corners and far across a wide plain
and back again whenever it wants.

Other cars can be all those other colors
the pink car doesn't care they can be loud and big
the pink car doesn't care that is why it can roll
so quietly and go slow until it goes fast for a while.

Other cars might honk their horns to seem big—
the pink car doesn't honk and doesn't worry
it just goes along the pale green lane
and around a sharp corner and down another lane
to stop in a special spot. Why is the spot special?
Because the pink car stopped there!

Stopping quiet but ready to go, to go
and be the pink car which is all it wants.
And when will I, when can
I ever be the man
implied by that sedan?

# Suzanne Cleary

I most remember the class where we lie
on our backs, on the cold floor, eyes closed, listening
to a story set in tall grasses, a land of flash floods.
Ten babies slept in a wagon as a stream risen from nothing
trampled like white horses toward them.
We heard the horses, pulling their terrible silence.
Then he asked us to open our eyes. Our teacher
took from his pocket an orange square, dropped it:
this had wrapped one of the babies.
This was found after the water receded.

I remember the woman with red hair
kneeling before the scarf, afraid to touch it,
our teacher telling her she could stop
by saying, *OK, Good.*
I remember the boy named Michael, who
once told me he loved me. Michael
approached with tiny steps, heel to toe,
as if he were measuring land,
and, all at once, he fell
on the scarf. It could have been funny,
loud, clumsy. Another context, another moment,
it would have been ridiculous.
Head down, he held the scarf to his eyes.

My turn, I didn't move. I stared
at the orange scarf, but not as long
as I'd have liked to, for this was a class
and there were others in line for their grief.
I touched it, lightly, with one hand,
folded it into a square, a smaller square, smaller.

What is lived in a life?
Our teacher making up that story
as he watched us lie on the dusty floor,
our rising, one by one,
to play with loss, to practice,
what is *lived, to live*? What was that desire
to move through ourselves to the orange
cotton, agreed upon, passed
from one to another?

# Leanne O'Sullivan

I used to lie on the floor for hours after
school with the phone cradled between
my shoulder and my ear, a plate of cold
rice to my left, my school books to my right.
Twirling the cord between my fingers
I spoke to friends who recognised the
language of our realm. Throats and lungs
swollen, we talked into the heart of the night,
toying with the idea of hair dye and suicide,
about the boys who didn't love us,
who we loved too much, the pang
of the nights. Each sentence was
new territory, like a door someone was
rushing into, the glass shattering
with delirium, with knowledge and fear.
My Mother never complained about the phone bill,
what it cost for her daughter to disappear
behind a door, watching the cord
stretching its muscle away from her.
Perhaps she thought it was the only way
she could reach me, sending me away
to speak in the underworld.
As long as I was speaking
she could put my ear to the tenuous earth
and allow me to listen, to decipher.

And these were the elements of my Mother,
the earthed wire, the burning cable,
as if she flowed into the room with
me to somehow say, Stay where I can reach you,
the dim room, the dark earth. Speak of this
and when you feel removed from it
I will pull the cord and take you
back towards me.

# Mark Halliday

How do I feel about "There's a Moon Out Tonight"
by the Capris?
I thought you'd never ask.

Marcia Koomen lived across Cherry Lane
getting tall, taller than me in fifth grade
and smiling behind her glasses, she knew something.
The summer nights in Raleigh were thick
with something bright in the dark; you could ride
bikes under the moon and in and out of
lampshine at the corner of Wade and Dogwood,
not caring about touching a girl, or, later,
not caring much still but happy to be a boy
who could some day "have" a girl, and conscious of
a shivering beauty caught in the word *girl*

*There's a girl at my side*
*that I adore*
                —the Capris knew something all together
and it called for this new verb, to adore;
something out there ahead of my bicycle in the dark;
I cared a lot about Paladin on "Have Gun—Will Travel"
but did I adore him? Scotty Koomen, years older,
got sort of pale and brittle when he went to visit

a certain girl in his class, he seemed to have trouble
breathing . . .

> There's a glow in my heart
> I never felt before

—not exactly in my heart yet but it was
what *would* be there if I rode just maybe deeper down
Dogwood Lane in the busy dark.

Across Dogwood lived Ann Dailey
who had freckles and an awesome kind of largeness,
not fat but big and this made my eyes feel hot and burny;
she moved slowly doing chores in her yard,
her long tanning thighs seemed sarcastic
as if she knew soon her freckled beauty must positively
carry her somehow out, out and away . . . And
Shelby Wilson one night kissed her on the lips.
I saw it happen—on the sofa in the basement—
her folks weren't home. Right on the lips!

Amazing lips are in your future, boy. That's
what the Capris were telling me; the North Carolina moon
is natural and it can find you anywhere:
you have to let the moon paint you and your bike
and the picture of Elvis in your pocket

and it shines down on Marcia's hair
and on the thought of the green eyes of Ann Dailey.
Ride and wait, wait and watch;
you laugh, you shiver in the summer-cool-dark,
you speak of the Yankees and the Pirates but
cut a side glance at Marcia's tall shape
but when she says anything serious exasperate her
yelling Little Richard's wop bop alu bop

but this dodging, dodging will end—
somewhere—
the Capris being on Marcia's side.
*Baby, I never felt this way before*
*I guess it's because there's a moon out tonight*

and once that shining starts
no amount of irony will ever quite ride the Capris out of
    town.
I picture a deep pool with yellow flowers drifting
on the surface. The song pours up
out of that pool.

*Shoshauna Shy*

My lemon-colored
whisper-weight blouse
with keyhole closure
and sweetheart neckline is tucked
into a pastel silhouette skirt
with side-slit vents
and triplicate pleats
when I realize in the sunlight
through the windshield
that the cool yellow of this blouse clashes
with the buttermilk heather in my skirt
which makes me slightly queasy
however

the periwinkle in the pattern on the sash
is sufficiently echoed by the twill uppers
of my buckle-snug sandals
while the accents on my purse
pick up the pink
in the button stitches

and then as we pass
through Weapons Check

it's reassuring to note
how the yellows momentarily mesh
and make an overall pleasing
composite

# Stephen Dunn

## ON THE DEATH OF A COLLEAGUE | 010

She taught theater, so we gathered
in the theater.
We praised her voice, her knowledge,
how good she was
with *Godot* and just four months later
with *Gigi*.
She was fifty. The problem in the liver.
Each of us recalled
an incident in which she'd been kind
or witty.
I told about being unable to speak
from my diaphragm
and how she made me lie down, placed her hand
where the failure was
and showed me how to breathe.
But afterwards
I only could do it when I lay down
and that became a joke
between us, and I told it as my offering
to the audience.
I was on stage and I heard myself
wishing to be impressive.
Someone else spoke of her cats
and no one spoke
of her face or the last few parties.

The fact was
I had avoided her for months.

It was a student's turn to speak, a sophomore,
one of her actors.
She was a drunk, he said, often came to class
reeking.
Sometimes he couldn't look at her, the blotches,
the awful puffiness.
And yet she was a great teacher,
he loved her,
but thought someone should say
what everyone knew
because she didn't die by accident.

Everyone was crying. Everyone was crying and it
was almost over now.
The remaining speaker, an historian, said he'd cut
his speech short.
And the Chairman stood up as if by habit,
said something about loss
and thanked us for coming. None of us moved
except some students
to the student who'd spoken, and then others
moved to him, across dividers,
down aisles, to his side of the stage.

## Sharon Olds

On the ten-below-zero day, it was on,
near the patients' chair, the old heater
kept by the analyst's couch, at the end,
like the infant's headstone that was added near the foot
of my father's grave. And it was hot, with the almost
laughing satire of a fire's heat,
the little coils like hairs in Hell.
And it was making a group of sick noises—
I wanted the doctor to turn it off
but I couldn't seem to ask, so I just
stared, but it did not budge. The doctor
turned his heavy, soft palm
outward, toward me, inviting me to speak, I
said, "If you're cold—are you cold? But if it's on
for me . . ." He held his palm out toward me,
I tried to ask, but I only muttered,
but he said, "Of course," as if I had asked,
and he stood and approached the heater, and then
stood on one foot, and threw himself
toward the wall with one hand, and with the other hand
reached down, behind the couch, to pull
the plug out. I looked away,
I had not known he would have to bend
like that. And I was so moved, that he
would act undignified, to help me,

that I cried, not trying to stop, but as if
the moans made sentences which bore
some human message. If he would cast himself toward the
outlet for me, as if bending with me in my old
shame and horror, then I would rest
on his art—and the heater purred, like a creature
or the familiar of a creature, or the child of a familiar,
the father of a child, the spirit of a father,
the healing of a spirit, the vision of healing,
the heat of vision, the power of the heat,
the pleasure of the power.

# Mary Cornish

I like the generosity of numbers.
The way, for example,
they are willing to count
anything or anyone:
two pickles, one door to the room,
eight dancers dressed as swans.

I like the domesticity of addition—
*add two cups of milk and stir—*
the sense of plenty: six plums
on the ground, three more
falling from the tree.

And multiplication's school
of fish times fish,
whose silver bodies breed
beneath the shadow
of a boat.

Even subtraction is never loss,
just addition somewhere else:
five sparrows take away two,
the two in someone else's
garden now.

There's an amplitude to long division,
as it opens Chinese take-out
box by paper box,
inside every folded cookie
a new fortune.

And I never fail to be surprised
by the gift of an odd remainder,
footloose at the end:
forty-seven divided by eleven equals four,
with three remaining.

Three boys beyond their mothers' call,
two Italians off to the sea,
one sock that isn't anywhere you look.

# Martha Collins

Draw a line. Write a line. There.
Stay in line, hold the line, a glance
between the lines is fine but don't
turn corners, cross, cut in, go over
or out, between two points of no
return's a line of flight, between
two points of view's a line of vision.
But a line of thought is rarely
straight, an open line's no party
line, however fine your point.
A line of fire communicates, but drop
your weapons and drop your line,
consider the shortest distance from $x$
to $y$, let $x$ be me, let $y$ be you.

## Miller Williams

I threw a snowball across the backyard.
My dog ran after it to bring it back.
It broke as it fell, scattering snow over snow.
She stood confused, seeing and smelling nothing.
She searched in widening circles until I called her.

She looked at me and said as clearly in silence
as if she had spoken,
I know it's here, I'll find it,
went back to the center and started the circles again.

I called her two more times before she came
slowly, stopping once to look back.

That was this morning. I'm sure that she's forgotten.
I've had some trouble putting it out of my mind.

# Mark Jarman

1.
Dear God, Our Heavenly Father, Gracious Lord,
Mother Love and Maker, Light Divine,
Atomic Fingertip, Cosmic Design,
First Letter of the Alphabet, Last Word,
Mutual Satisfaction, Cash Award,
Auditor Who Approves Our Bottom Line,
Examiner Who Says That We Are Fine,
Oasis That All Sands Are Running Toward.

I can say almost anything about you,
O Big Idea, and with each epithet,
Create new reasons to believe or doubt you,
Black Hole, White Hole, Presidential Jet.
But what's the anything I must leave out? You
Solve nothing but the problems that I set.

## Leroy V. Quintana

POEM FOR SALT | 016

The biggest snowstorm to hit Denver in twenty years.
What is the world to do, freed from the shackles
of the eight hours needed to earn its daily salary?

Only on a day such as this does salt overshadow gold.
Salt, with its lips of blue fire, common as gossip,
ordinary as sin. Like true love and gasoline,
missed only when they run out. Salt spilling
from a blue container a young girl is holding,
along with an umbrella, on the label of a blue
container of salt that the woman across the street,
under her umbrella is pouring behind her left rear wheel,
to no avail this discontented, unbuttoned December
       morning.

## Mary Ruefle

**THE HAND | 017**

The teacher asks a question.
You know the answer, you suspect
you are the only one in the classroom
who knows the answer, because the person
in question is yourself, and on that
you are the greatest living authority,
but you don't raise your hand.
You raise the top of your desk
and take out an apple.
You look out the window.
You don't raise your hand and there is
some essential beauty in your fingers,
which aren't even drumming, but lie
flat and peaceful.
The teacher repeats the question.
Outside the window, on an overhanging branch,
a robin is ruffling its feathers
and spring is in the air.

## Dan Brown

I was in Princeton of all
Places. My ninth grade class
Was there on a field trip: the usual
Shepherding from edifice
To edifice—a lot of gray
Stone—winding up, though,
With something a little out of the way:
The opportunity to view
A classic three-acter
At the U's own theater.

The play I don't remember much
About: your basic exercise
In wigs and bodices and such.
The memorable thing was
The curtain call. How the one
Coming out was a grim guy
In tweed and tie. How the lone
Lifting of his palm by
Itself extinguished the applause.
How he had "terrible news"—

But not the news I feared. Not
Where to go. Not how
To get there. Not what

To do when you got there—go
Sit against a wall, put
Your head down, clasp your hands
Behind your head, you might shut
Your eyes in case the world ends—
None of that. Maybe he
Was finding it decidedly

Hard to get the words out,
But what the words amounted to
Wasn't the worst thing: not
Anything that had to do
With going up in a solar hell,
But rather with the President,
A motorcade, a hospital—
With how the evident extent
Of anybody's sudden death
Was elsewhere and over with.

# Rebecca Wee

## HOOP SNAKE | 019

**Any of several snakes, such as the mud snake, said to grasp
the tail in the mouth and move with a rolling, hooplike motion.**

—*American Heritage Dictionary of the English Language*

the second time we met
he told me about the hoop snake

(temporal, exquisite,
a godless man

so I listened)

we weren't sure though
if it could be true

a snake that takes its tail in its mouth,
then rolls through the world

but there are reasons to believe in god
and this seems a good one

we brought wine to the porch, spoke
of piety, marriage,

devotion assumed for reasons
that could not sustain it

while lightning took apart the sky
the fields leapt up the stream's

muddy lustre its sinuous length
liminal, lush, the grass black

the unheard melodies and those that catch
the leaves beginning to fret

I don't remember now what he said his eyes
revising that dark

after he left I walked through the grass the rain
asked *how do things work?*

we are after something miraculous

we open our mouths we believe
we turn
at times

we gather speed

# Charles Simic

## BESTIARY FOR THE FINGERS
## OF MY RIGHT HAND | 020


1.

Thumb, loose tooth of a horse.
Rooster to his hens.
Horn of a devil. Fat worm
They have attached to my flesh
At the time of my birth.
It takes four to hold him down,
Bend him in half, until the bone
Begins to whimper.

Cut him off. He can take care
Of himself. Take root in the earth,
Or go hunting with wolves.


2.

The second points the way.
True way. The path crosses the earth,
The moon and some stars.
Watch, he points further.
He points to himself.


3.

The middle one has backache.
Stiff, still unaccustomed to this life;

An old man at birth. It's about something
That he had and lost,
That he looks for within my hand,
The way a dog looks
For fleas
With a sharp tooth.

4.
The fourth is mystery.
Sometimes as my hand
Rests on the table
He jumps by himself
As though someone called his name.

After each bone, finger,
I come to him, troubled.

5.
Something stirs in the fifth
Something perpetually at the point
Of birth. Weak and submissive,
His touch is gentle.
It weighs a tear.
It takes the mote out of the eye.

## Geraldine Connolly

The turquoise pool rose up to meet us,
its slide a silver afterthought down which
we plunged, screaming, into a mirage of bubbles.
We did not exist beyond the gaze of a boy.

Shaking water off our limbs, we lifted
up from ladder rungs across the fern-cool
lip of rim. Afternoon. Oiled and sated,
we sunbathed, rose and paraded the concrete,

danced to the low beat of "Duke of Earl."
Past cherry colas, hot-dogs, Dreamsicles,
we came to the counter where bees staggered
into root beer cups and drowned. We gobbled

cotton candy torches, sweet as furtive kisses,
shared on benches beneath summer shadows.
Cherry. Elm. Sycamore. We spread our chenille
blankets across grass, pressed radios to our ears,

mouthing the old words, then loosened
thin bikini straps and rubbed baby oil with iodine
across sunburned shoulders, tossing a glance
through the chain link at an improbable world.

# Tom Wayman

Nothing. When we realized you weren't here
we sat with our hands folded on our desks
in silence, for the full two hours

>  Everything, I gave an exam worth
>  40 percent of the grade for this term
>  and assigned some reading due today
>  on which I'm about to hand out a quiz
>  worth 50 percent

Nothing. None of the content of this course
has value or meaning
Take as many days off as you like:
any activities we undertake as a class
I assure you will not matter either to you or me
and are without purpose

>  Everything. A few minutes after we began last time
>  a shaft of light suddenly descended and an angel
>  or other heavenly being appeared
>  and revealed to us what each woman or man must do
>  to attain divine wisdom in this life and
>  the hereafter
>  This is the last time the class will meet

before we disperse to bring the good news to all people
    on earth

Nothing. When you are not present
how could something significant occur?

    Everything. Contained in this classroom
    is a microcosm of human experience
    assembled for you to query and examine and ponder
    This is not the only place such an opportunity has been
        gathered

    but it was one place

    And you weren't here

## Kevin Young

To watch you walk
cross the room in your black

corduroys is to see
civilization start—

the *wish-*
*whish-whisk*

of your strut is flint
striking rock—the spark

of a length of cord
rubbed till

smoke starts—you stir
me like coal

and for days smoulder.
I am no more

a Boy Scout and, besides,
could never

put you out—you
keep me on

all day like an iron, out
of habit—

you threaten, brick-
house, to burn

all this down. You leave me
only a chimney.

# G. E. Patterson

I had everything and luck: Rings of smoke
blown for me; sunlight safe inside the leaves
of cottonwoods; pure, simple harmonies
of church music, echoes of slave songs; scraps
of candy wrappers—airborne. Everything.
Mother and father, brother, aunts, uncles;
chores and schoolwork and playtime. Everything.

I was given gloves against winter cold.
I was made to wear gloves when I gardened.
I was made to garden; taught to hold forks
in my left hand when cutting, in my right
when bringing food to my mouth. Everything.

I had clothes I was told not to wear outside;
a face you could clean up almost handsome;
I had friends to fight with and secrets, spread
all over the neighborhood; the best teachers,
white and colored. I'm not making this up.
I knew that I had everything. Still do.

# Richard Jones

I have been studying the difference
between solitude and loneliness,
telling the story of my life
to the clean white towels taken warm from the dryer.
I carry them through the house
as though they were my children
asleep in my arms.

# Kenneth Koch

I love you as a sheriff searches for a walnut
That will solve a murder case unsolved for years
Because the murderer left it in the snow beside a window
Through which he saw her head, connecting with
Her shoulders by a neck, and laid a red
Roof in her heart. For this we live a thousand years;
For this we love, and we live because we love, we are not
Inside a bottle, thank goodness! I love you as a
Kid searches for a goat; I am crazier than shirttails
In the wind, when you're near, a wind that blows from
The big blue sea, so shiny so deep and so unlike us;
I think I am bicycling across an Africa of green and white
 fields
Always, to be near you, even in my heart
When I'm awake, which swims, and also I believe that you
Are trustworthy as the sidewalk which leads me to
The place where I again think of you, a new
Harmony of thoughts! I love you as the sunlight leads the
 prow
Of a ship which sails
From Hartford to Miami, and I love you
Best at dawn, when even before I am awake the sun
Receives me in the questions which you always pose.

I don't know what it is,
but I distrust myself
when I start to like a girl
    a lot.

It makes me nervous.
I don't say the right things
or perhaps I start
    to examine,

                evaluate

                      compute

    what I am saying.

If I say, "Do you think it's going to rain?"
and she says, "I don't know,"
I start thinking: Does she really like me?

In other words
I get a little creepy.

A friend of mine once said,
"It's twenty times better to be friends
    with someone
than it is to be in love with them."

I think he's right and besides,
it's raining somewhere, programming flowers
and keeping snails happy.
       That's all taken care of.

              BUT
if a girl likes me a lot
and starts getting real nervous
and suddenly begins asking me funny questions
and looks sad if I give the wrong answers
and she says things like,
"Do you think it's going to rain?"
and I say, "It beats me,"
and she says, "Oh,"
and looks a little sad
at the clear blue California sky,
I think: Thank God, it's you, baby, this time
       instead of me.

# David Kirby

## MODERATION KILLS (EXCUSEZ-MOI, JE SUIS SICK AS A DOG) | 028

I'm tackling this particularly chewy piece of sushi and
      recalling the only Japanese words I know,
"Fugu wa kuitashii, inochi wa oshishii," meaning,
      "I would like to eat fugu—but live!"
which, I've read, is something Japanese executives say
      when contemplating a particularly risky

course of action, because whereas the testes of the fugu
      or blowfish are harmless
yet highly prized as a virility builder, the liver,
      which is almost identical
in appearance to the testes, *is* toxic, so that
      a less-cautious individual,

a fisherman, say, who thinks himself as skillful
      as the chef who has actually been
educated and licensed in the preparation of fugu,
      might eat the wrong organ and die,
face-down in his rice bowl, chopsticks nipping
      spasmodically at the air.

Coming in from the vegetable patch, the fisherman's wife
      sees him cooling in the remains
of his meal and shrieks, and I don't know
      the Japanese for this,

"You have eaten fugu—and died!" True, though
        for anyone other than the new widow,

why should his death be exclaimed upon as though
        it were a failure or defeat,
since the fisherman had finished a good day of work
        and was not only enjoying his tasty snack
but also looking forward to the enhancement
        of his powers of generation,
this being therefore a fine moment in which to expire
        and certainly preferable to
countless moments of life as a fumbling drooler
        (since fugu liver can paralyze
as well), a burden to his loved ones as well as
        the object of their contempt.

Then someone across the table from me says he's *heard*
        of a state of mind called boredom
but never actually experienced it, and I wonder,
        Can a mind that never sinks
into the cold gray waters of boredom ever rise to
        the blue-and-gold heavens of ecstasy?

Then someone else shouts, "Excusez-moi, je suis sick
        as a dog!" and disappears

laughing, but that's okay, because "ecstasy" =
      "ex stasis" = "get off the dime" =
"fish or cut bait" = "lead, follow, or get out
      of the way," does it not?


Besides, who's to say the fisherman didn't hate
      his wife, couldn't stand her?
And had to eat fugu testes in order to be able
      to countenance her and
therefore is better off dead and unknowing than
      alive and fully sentient of such misery?


Or hated himself and therefore is better off dead, etc.?
      And therefore who is
more admirable, the executive who fears death
      or the fisherman who actually dies?
Does the former feel brave merely because
      he has *talked* of taking a risk?


Would the doughty fisherman have said "Fugu wa kuitashii,
      inochi wa oshishii" and taken pride
in his temperance? Certainly not—
      offered the same challenge under identical
circumstances, he'd have said, and I don't know
      the Japanese for this either, "Moderation kills."

# Carol Ann Duffy

## MRS MIDAS | 029

It was late September. I'd just poured a glass of wine, begun
to unwind, while the vegetables cooked. The kitchen
filled with the smell of itself, relaxed, its steamy breath
gently blanching the windows. So I opened one,
then with my fingers wiped the other's glass like a brow.
He was standing under the pear tree snapping a twig.

Now the garden was long and the visibility poor, the way
the dark of the ground seems to drink the light of the sky,
but that twig in his hand was gold. And then he plucked
a pear from a branch—we grew Fondante d'Automne—
and it sat in his palm like a light bulb. On.
I thought to myself, Is he putting fairy lights in the tree?

He came into the house. The doorknobs gleamed.
He drew the blinds. You know the mind; I thought of
the Field of the Cloth of Gold and of Miss Macready.
He sat in that chair like a king on a burnished throne.
The look on his face was strange, wild, vain. I said,
What in the name of God is going on? He started to laugh.

I served up the meal. For starters, corn on the cob.
Within seconds he was spitting out the teeth of the rich.
He toyed with his spoon, then mine, then with the knives,
     the forks.

He asked where was the wine. I poured with a shaking
    hand,
a fragrant, bone-dry white from Italy, then watched
as he picked up the glass, goblet, golden chalice, drank.

It was then that I started to scream. He sank to his knees.
After we'd both calmed down, I finished the wine
on my own, hearing him out. I made him sit
on the other side of the room and keep his hands to
    himself.
I locked the cat in the cellar. I moved the phone.
The toilet I didn't mind. I couldn't believe my ears:

how he'd had a wish. Look, we all have wishes; granted.
But who has wishes granted? Him. Do you know about
    gold?
It feeds no one; aurum, soft, untarnishable; slakes
no thirst. He tried to light a cigarette; I gazed, entranced,
as the blue flame played on its luteous stem. At least,
I said, you'll be able to give up smoking for good.

Separate beds. In fact, I put a chair against my door,
near petrified. He was below, turning the spare room
into the tomb of Tutankhamun. You see, we were passionate
    then,

in those halcyon days; unwrapping each other, rapidly,
like presents, fast food. But now I feared his honeyed
    embrace,
the kiss that would turn my lips to a work of art.

And who, when it comes to the crunch, can live
with a heart of gold? That night, I dreamt I bore
his child, its perfect ore limbs, its little tongue
like a precious latch, its amber eyes
holding their pupils like flies. My dream-milk
burned in my breasts. I woke to the streaming sun.

So he had to move out. We'd a caravan
in the wilds, in a glade of its own. I drove him up
under cover of dark. He sat in the back.
And then I came home, the woman who married the fool
who wished for gold. At first I visited, odd times,
parking the car a good way off, then walking.

You knew you were getting close. Golden trout
on the grass. One day, a hare hung from a larch,
a beautiful lemon mistake. And then his footprints,
glistening next to the river's path. He was thin,
delirious; hearing, he said, the music of Pan
from the woods. Listen. That was the last straw.

What gets me now is not the idiocy or greed
but lack of thought for me. Pure selfishness. I sold
the contents of the house and came down here.
I think of him in certain lights, dawn, late afternoon,
and once a bowl of apples stopped me dead. I miss most,
even now, his hands, his warm hands on my skin, his touch.

# Larry Levis

## THE OLDEST LIVING
## THING IN L.A. | 030

At Wilshire & Santa Monica I saw an opossum
Trying to cross the street. It was late, the street
Was brightly lit, the opossum would take
A few steps forward, then back away from the breath
Of moving traffic. People coming out of the bars
Would approach, as if to help it somehow.
It would lift its black lips & show them
The reddened gums, the long rows of incisors,
Teeth that went all the way back beyond
The flames of Troy & Carthage, beyond sheep
Grazing rock-strewn hills, fragments of ruins
In the grass at San Vitale. It would back away
Delicately & smoothly, stepping carefully
As it always had. It could mangle someone's hand
In twenty seconds. Mangle it for good. It could
Sever it completely from the wrist in forty.
There was nothing to be done for it. Someone
Or other probably called the LAPD, who then
Called Animal Control, who woke a driver, who
Then dressed in mailed gloves, the kind of thing
Small knights once wore into battle, who gathered
Together his pole with a noose on the end,
A light steel net to snare it with, someone who hoped
The thing would have vanished by the time he got there.

# Li-Young Lee

I buried my father
in the sky.
Since then, the birds
clean and comb him every morning
and pull the blanket up to his chin
every night.

I buried my father underground.
Since then, my ladders
only climb down,
and all the earth has become a house
whose rooms are the hours, whose doors
stand open at evening, receiving
guest after guest.
Sometimes I see past them
to the tables spread for a wedding feast.

I buried my father in my heart.
Now he grows in me, my strange son,
my little root who won't drink milk,
little pale foot sunk in unheard-of night,
little clock spring newly wet
in the fire, little grape, parent to the future
wine, a son the fruit of his own son,
little father I ransom with my life.

# Bob Hicok

Chairs move by themselves, and books.
Grandchildren visit, stand
new and nameless, their faces' puzzles
missing pieces. She's like a fish

in deep ocean, its body made of light.
She floats through rooms, through
my eyes, an old woman bereft
of chronicle, the parable of her life.

And though she's almost a child
there's still blood between us:
I passed through her to arrive.
So I protect her from knives,

stairs, from the street that calls
as rivers do, a summons to walk away,
to follow. And dress her,
demonstrate how buttons work,

when she sometimes looks up
and says my name, the sound arriving
like the trill of a bird so rare
it's rumored no longer to exist.

# Marianne Boruch

An eagle and a squirrel. A bull and a sage.
All take two hands, even the sheep
whose mouth is a lever for nothing, neither
grass nor complaint. The black swan's
mostly one long arm, bent
at the elbow but there's always feathers
to fool with. Front leaf: a boy
with a candle, leaning curious while
an old man makes
a Shakespeare. The small pointed beard
is a giveaway.

        I always wanted to, especially
because of the candle part. How the eye is finally
a finger bent to make an emptiness. Or that
a thing thrown up there
is worlds bigger than how it starts. So I liked
the ceiling better than the wall, looking up
where stars roamed and moon sometimes
hovered, were the roof lost,
were we lucky
and forgot ourselves.

# Ronald Koertge

They were never handsome and often came
with a hormone imbalance manifested by corpulence,
a yodel of a voice or ears big as kidneys.

But each was brave. More than once a sidekick
has thrown himself in front of our hero in order
to receive the bullet or blow meant for that
perfect face and body.

Thankfully, heroes never die in movies and leave
the sidekick alone. He would not stand for it.
Gabby or Pat, Pancho or Andy remind us of a part
of ourselves,

the dependent part that can never grow up,
the part that is painfully eager to please,
always wants a hug and never gets enough.

Who could sit in a darkened theatre, listen
to the organ music and watch the best
of ourselves lowered into the ground while
the rest stood up there, tears pouring off
that enormous nose.

# William Matthews

I read to the entire plebe class,
in two batches. Twice the hall filled
with bodies dressed alike, each toting
a copy of my book. What would my
shrink say, if I had one, about
such a dream, if it were a dream?

Question-and-answer time.
"Sir," a cadet yelled from the balcony,
and gave his name and rank, and then,
closing his parentheses, yelled
"Sir" again. "Why do your poems give
me a headache when I try

to understand them?" he asked. "Do
you want that?" I have a gift for
gentle jokes to defuse tension,
but this was not the time to use it.
"I try to write as well as I can
what it feels like to be human,"

I started, picking my way care-
fully, for he and I were, after
all, pained by the same dumb longings.

"I try to say what I don't know
how to say, but of course I can't
get much of it down at all."

By now I was sweating bullets.
"I don't want my poems to be hard,
unless the truth is, if there is
a truth." Silence hung in the hall
like a heavy fabric. Now my
head ached. "Sir," he yelled. "Thank you. Sir."

# Dean Young

Because it seems the only way to save the roses
is to pluck the Japanese beetles out of
their convoluted paradise
and kill them, I think for a moment,
instead of crushing them in the driveway,
of impaling them on the thorns.
Perhaps they'd prefer that.

## Cornelius Eady

Some folks will tell you the blues is a woman,
Some type of supernatural creature.
My mother would tell you, if she could,
About her life with my father,
A strange and sometimes cruel gentleman.
She would tell you about the choices
A young black woman faces.
Is falling in love with some man
A deal with the devil
In blue terms, the tongue we use
When we don't want nuance
To get in the way,
When we need to talk straight.
My mother chooses my father
After choosing a man
Who was, as we sing it,
Of no account.
This man made my father look good,
That's how bad it was.
He made my father seem like an island
In the middle of a stormy sea,
He made my father look like a rock.
And is the blues the moment you realize
You exist in a stacked deck,
You look in a mirror at your young face,

The face my sister carries,
And you know it's the only leverage
You've got.
Does this create a hurt that whispers
How you going to do?
Is the blues the moment
You shrug your shoulders
And agree, a girl without money
Is nothing, dust
To be pushed around by any old breeze.
Compared to this,
My father seems, briefly,
To be a fire escape.
This is the way the blues works
Its sorry wonders,
Makes trouble look like
A feather bed,
Makes the wrong man's kisses
A healing.

# Peter Meinke

When I was young and shiny as an apple in the good Lord's
       garden
I loved a woman whose beauty like the moon moved all the
       humming heavens to music
till the stars with their tiny teeth burst into song
and I fell on the ground before her while the sky hardened
and she laughed and turned me down softly, I was so
       young.

When I was a man sharp as a polished axe in the polleny
       orchard
I loved a woman whose perfume swayed in the air, turning
       the modest flowers scarlet and loose
till the jonquils opened their throats and cackled out loud
when I broke my hand on her door and cried I was tortured
and she laughed and refused me, only one man in a crowd.

When I grew old, owning more than my share of the
       garden,
I loved a woman young and fresh as a larkspur trembling
       in the morning's translucent coolness,
her eyes had seen nothing but good, and as the sun's gold
rolled off her wrists with reluctance, she pardoned
my foolishness, laughed and turned me down gently, I was
       so old.

And when I fell ill, rooted in a damp house spotted with
     curses,
I loved a woman whose bones rustled like insect wings
     through the echoing darkening rooms
and the ceiling dropped like a gardener's hoe toward my
     bed
so I stretched out my hand to her begging my god for mercy
and she laughed and embraced me sweetly, I was so dead.

## Yves Bonnefoy

### PASSER-BY, THESE ARE
### WORDS . . . | 039

Passer-by, these are words. But instead of reading
      I want you to listen: to this frail
      Voice like that of letters eaten by grass.

Lend an ear, hear first of all the happy bee
Foraging in our almost rubbed-out names.
      It flits between two sprays of leaves,
Carrying the sound of branches that are real
      To those that filigree the still unseen.

Then know an even fainter sound, and let it be
      The endless murmuring of all our shades.
Their whisper rises from beneath the stones
      To fuse into a single heat with that blind
      Light you are as yet, who can still gaze.

      May your listening be good! Silence
Is a threshold where a twig breaks in your hand,
      Imperceptibly, as you attempt to disengage
      A name upon a stone:

And so our absent names untangle your alarms.
      And for you who move away, pensively,
      Here becomes there without ceasing to be.

# Jim Daniels

My brother kept
in a frame on the wall
pictures of every motorcycle, car, truck:
in his rusted out Impala convertible
wearing his cap and gown
waving
in his yellow Barracuda
with a girl leaning into him
waving
on his Honda 350
waving
on his Honda 750 with the boys
holding a beer
waving
in his first rig
wearing a baseball hat backwards
waving
in his Mercury Montego
getting married
waving
in his black LTD
trying to sell real estate
waving
back to driving trucks
a shiny new rig

waving
on his Harley Sportster
with his wife on the back
waving
his son in a car seat
with his own steering wheel
my brother leaning over him
in an old Ford pickup
and they are
waving
holding a wrench a rag
a hose a shammy
waving.

My brother helmetless
rides off on his Harley
waving
my brother's feet
rarely touch the ground—
waving waving
face pressed to the wind
no camera to save him.

# Naomi Shihab Nye

## RAIN | 041

A teacher asked Paul
what he would remember
from third grade, and he sat
a long time before writing
"this year sumbody tutched me
on the sholder"
and turned his paper in.
Later she showed it to me
as an example of her wasted life.
The words he wrote were large
as houses in a landscape.
He wanted to go inside them
and live, he could fill in
the windows of "o" and "d"
and be safe while outside
birds building nests in drainpipes
knew nothing of the coming rain.

## Yannis Ritsos

### A MYOPIC CHILD | 042

The other kids romped around the playground; their voices
rose up to the roofs of the quarter, also the "splock" of their
    ball
like a globular world, all joy and impertinence.

But he was reading the whole time, there in the spring
    window,
within a rectangle of bitter silence,
until he finally fell asleep on the window sill in the
    afternoon,
oblivious to the voices of those his own age
and to premature fears of his own superiority.

The glasses on his nose looked like
a little bike left leaning against a tree,
off in a far-flung, light-flooded countryside,
a bike of some child who had died.

the people are very small and shrink,
dwarves on the way to netsuke hell
bound for a flea circus in full
retreat toward sub-atomic particles—
difficult to keep in focus, the figures
at that end are nearly indistinguishable,
generals at the heads of minute armies
differing little from fishwives,
emperors the same as eskimos
huddled under improvisations of snow—
eskimos, though, now have the advantage,
for it seems to be freezing there, a climate
which might explain the population's
*outré* dress, their period costumes
of felt and silk and eiderdown,
their fur concoctions stuffed with straw
held in place with flexible strips of bark,
and all to no avail, the midgets forever
stamping their match-stick feet,
blowing on the numb flagella of their fingers—
but wait, bring a light, clean the lens . . .
can it be those shivering arms are waving,
are trying to attract attention, hailing you?

seen from the other end of the telescope,
your eye must appear enormous,
must fill the sky like a sun,
and as you occupy their tiny heads
naturally they wish to communicate,
to tell you of their diminishing perspective—
        yes, look again, their hands are cupped
around the pinholes of their mouths,
their faces are swollen, red with effort;
why, they're screaming fit to burst,
though what they say is anybody's guess,
it is next to impossible to hear them,
and most of them speak languages
for which no Rosetta stone can be found—
        but listen harder, use your imagination . . .
the people at the other end of the telescope,
are they trying to tell you their names?
yes, surely that must be it, their names
and those of those they love, and possibly
something else, some of them . . . listen . . .
the largest are struggling to explain
what befell them, how it happened
that they woke one morning as if adrift,

their moorings cut in the night,
and were swept out over the horizon,
borne on an ebbing tide and soon
to be discernible only as distance,
collapsed into mirage, made to become
legendary creatures now off every map.

# Lucille Clifton

to my aunt blanche
who rolled from grass to driveway
into the street one sunday morning.
i was ten.          i had never seen
a human woman hurl her basketball
of a body into the traffic of the world.
Praise to the drivers who stopped in time.
Praise to the faith with which she rose
after some moments then slowly walked
sighing back to her family.
Praise to the arms which understood
little or nothing of what it meant
but welcomed her in without judgment,
accepting it all like children might,
like God.

## Thomas Lux

### THE MAN INTO WHOSE YARD YOU
### SHOULD NOT HIT YOUR BALL | 045

each day mowed
and mowed his lawn, his dry quarter-acre,
the machine slicing a wisp
from each blade's tip. Dust storms rose
around the roar, 6 p.m. every day,
spring, summer, fall. If he could mow
the snow he would.
On one side, his neighbors the cows
turned their backs to him
and did what they do to the grass.
Where he worked, I don't know,
but it set his jaw to: tight.
His wife a cipher, shoebox tissue,
a shattered apron. As if
into her head he drove a wedge of shale.
Years later, his daughter goes to jail.
Mow, mow, mow his lawn
gently down a decade's summers.
On his other side lived mine and me,
across a narrow pasture, often fallow—
a field of fly balls, the best part of childhood
and baseball. But if a ball crossed his line,
as one did in 1956,
and another in 1958,

it came back coleslaw—his lawnmower
ate it up, happy
to cut something, no matter
what the manual said
about foreign objects,
stones, or sticks.

## Edward Field

They say the ice will hold
so there I go,
forced to believe them by my act of trusting people,
stepping out on it,

and naturally it gaps open
and I, forced to carry on coolly
by my act of being imperturbable,
slide erectly into the water wearing my captain's helmet,
waving to the shore with a sad smile,
"Goodbye my darlings, goodbye dear one,"
as the ice meets again over my head with a click.

# Charles Simic

Seems like a long time
Since the waiter took my order.
Grimy little luncheonette,
The snow falling outside.

Seems like it has grown darker
Since I last heard the kitchen door
Behind my back
Since I last noticed
Anyone pass on the street.

A glass of ice-water
Keeps me company
At this table I chose myself
Upon entering.

And a longing,
Incredible longing
To eavesdrop
On the conversation
Of cooks.

# David Young

It's summer, 1956, in Maine, a camp resort
on Belgrade Lakes, and I am cleaning fish,
part of my job, along with luggage, firewood,
Sunday ice cream, waking everyone
by jogging around the island every morning
swinging a rattle I hold in front of me
to break the nightly spider threads.
Adlai Stevenson is being nominated,
but won't, again, beat Eisenhower,
sad fact I'm half aware of, steeped as I am
in Russian novels, bathing in the tea-
brown lake, startling a deer and chasing it by canoe
as it swims from the island to the mainland.
I'm good at cleaning fish: lake trout,
those beautiful deep swimmers, brown trout,
I can fillet them and take them to the cook
and the grateful fisherman may send a piece
back from his table to mine, a salute.
I clean in a swarm of yellow jackets,
sure they won't sting me, so they don't,
though they can't resist the fish, the slime,
the guts that drop into the bucket, they're mad
for meat, fresh death, they swarm around

whenever I work at this outdoor sink
with somebody's loving catch.
Later this summer we'll find their nest
and burn it one night with a blowtorch
applied to the entrance, the paper hotel
glowing with fire and smoke like a lantern,
full of the death-bees, hornets, whatever they are,
that drop like little coals
and an oily smoke that rolls through the trees
into the night of the last American summer
next to this one, 36 years away, to show me
time is a pomegranate, many-chambered,
nothing like what I thought.

## C. S. Lewis

The sky was low, the sounding rain was falling dense and
    dark,
And Noah's sons were standing at the window of the Ark.

The beasts were in, but Japhet said, 'I see one creature
    more
Belated and unmated there come knocking at the door.'

'Well let him knock,' said Ham, 'Or let him drown or
    learn to swim.
We're overcrowded as it is; we've got no room for him.'

'And yet it knocks, how terribly it knocks,' said Shem, 'Its
    feet
Are hard as horn—but oh the air that comes from it is
    sweet.'

'Now hush,' said Ham, 'You'll waken Dad, and once he
    comes to see
What's at the door, it's sure to mean more work for you
    and me.'

Noah's voice came roaring from the darkness down below,
'Some animal is knocking. Take it in before we go.'

Ham shouted back, and savagely he nudged the other two,
'That's only Japhet knocking down a brad-nail in his
    shoe.'

Said Noah, 'Boys, I hear a noise that's like a horse's hoof.'
Said Ham, 'Why, that's the dreadful rain that drums upon
    the roof.'

Noah tumbled up on deck and out he put his head;
His face went grey, his knees were loosed, he tore his
    beard and said,

'Look, look! It would not wait. It turns away. It takes its
    flight.
Fine work you've made of it, my sons, between you all to-
    night!

'Even if I could outrun it now, it would not turn again
—Not now. Our great discourtesy has earned its high
    disdain.

'Oh noble and unmated beast, my sons were all unkind;
In such a night what stable and what manger will you
    find?

'Oh golden hoofs, oh cataracts of mane, oh nostrils wide
With indignation! Oh the neck wave-arched, the lovely
     pride!

'Oh long shall be the furrows ploughed across the hearts of
     men
Before it comes to stable and to manger once again,

'And dark and crooked all the ways in which our race shall
     walk,
And shrivelled all their manhood like a flower with broken
     stalk,

'And all the world, oh Ham, may curse the hour when you
     were born;
Because of you the Ark must sail without the Unicorn.'

# Eamon Grennan

## ON A 3¹/₂ OZ. LESSER YELLOWLEGS, DEPARTED BOSTON AUGUST 28, SHOT MARTINIQUE SEPTEMBER 3 | 050

*for Phoebe Palmer*

Little brother, would I could
Make it so far, the whole globe
Curling to the quick of your wing.

You leave our minds lagging
With no word for this gallant
Fly-by-night, blind flight.

But ah, the shot: you clot
In a cloud of feathers, drop
Dead in a nest of text-books.

Now seasons migrate without you
Flying south. At the gunman's door
The sea-grapes plump and darken.

# Carol Snow

Near a shrine in Japan he'd swept the path
and then placed camellia blossoms there.

Or—we had no way of knowing—he'd swept the path
between fallen camellias.

# Connie Wanek

AFTER US | 052

**I don't know if we're in the beginning or in the final stage.**

*—Tomas Tranströmer*

Rain is falling through the roof.
And all that prospered under the sun,
the books that opened in the morning
and closed at night, and all day
turned their pages to the light;

the sketches of boats and strong forearms
and clever faces, and of fields
and barns, and of a bowl of eggs,
and lying across the piano
the silver stick of a flute; everything

invented and imagined,
everything whispered and sung,
all silenced by cold rain.

The sky is the color of gravestones.
The rain tastes like salt, and rises
in the streets like a ruinous tide.
We spoke of millions, of billions of years.
We talked and talked.

Then a drop of rain fell
into the sound hole of the guitar, another
onto the unmade bed. And after us,
the rain will cease or it will go on falling,
even upon itself.

# Don Paterson

In the same way that the mindless diamond keeps
one spark of the planet's early fires
trapped forever in its net of ice,
it's not love's later heat that poetry holds,
but the atom of the love that drew it forth
from the silence: so if the bright coal of his love
begins to smoulder, the poet hears his voice
suddenly forced, like a bar-room singer's—boastful
with his own huge feeling, or drowned by violins;
but if it yields a steadier light, he knows
the pure verse, when it finally comes, will sound
like a mountain spring, anonymous and serene.

Beneath the blue oblivious sky, the water
sings of nothing, not your name, not mine.

## Elizabeth Holmes

**THE FATHERS | 054**

**Captain Hook and Mr. Darling are traditionally played
by the same actor.**

Something's familiar about that villain
striding the deck of the *Jolly Roger,* chest
puffed out under the fancy jabot—
a bit like, yes, like Father huffing around
before an evening out, proper shirtfront
outthrust by an important bay window.
Particular about his cuff links as a pirate
about lace at his wrists. Same air of dashing
yet dastardly middle age. A penchant
for issuing orders and threats, and tying
up uncooperative dogs or Indian princesses.

No wonder we sons and daughters laugh
when Hook sits on the hot toadstool
over Peter's chimney, when Tinker Bell
flits out of his grasp. And especially
at his slapstick flailing through the sea,
pursued by that confident long-jawed beast,
time ticking loud in its belly.

# Reed Whittemore

On warm days in September the high school band
Is up with the birds and marches along our street,
Boom, boom,
To a field where it goes boom boom until eight forty-five
When it marches, as in the old rhyme, back, boom boom,
To its study halls, leaving our street
Empty except for the leaves that descend to no drum,
And lie still.
In September
A great many high school bands beat a great many drums,
And the silences after their partings are very deep.

# Richard Jones

In the tower the bell
is alone, like a man
in his room,
thinking and thinking.

The bell is made of iron.
It takes the weight
of a man
to make the bell move.

Far below, the bell feels
hands on a rope.
It considers this.
It turns its head.

Miles away,
a man in his room
hears the clear sound,
and lifts his head to listen.

## Lola Haskins

### DEARBORN NORTH APARTMENTS
### CHICAGO, ILLINOIS | 057

Rows of rectangles rise, set into brick.
And in every rectangle, there is a lamp.
Why should there be a lamp in every window?
Because in all this wide city, there is not
enough light. Because the young in the world
are crazy for light and the old are afraid
it will leave them. Because whoever you are,
if you come home late but it looks like noon,
you won't tense at the click as you walk in
which is probably after all only the heat
coming on, or the floorboards settling.
So when you fling your coat to its peg in
the hall, and kick off your heels, and unzip
your black velvet at that odd vee'd angle as if
someone were twisting your arm from behind,
then reach inside the closet for a hanger,
just to the dark left where the dresses live,
what happens next is a complete surprise.

# Chris Forhan

So this is what it's like when love
leaves, and one is disappointed
that the body and mind continue to exist,

exacting payment from each other,
engaging in stale rituals of desire,
and it would seem the best use of one's time

is not to stand for hours outside
her darkened house, drenched and chilled,
blinking into the slanting rain.

So this is what it's like to have to
practice amiability and learn
to say the orchard looks grand this evening

as the sun slips behind scumbled clouds
and the pears, mellowed to a golden-green,
glow like flames among the boughs.

It is now one claims there is comfort
in the constancy of nature, in the wind's way
of snatching dogwood blossoms from their branches,

scattering them in the dirt, in the slug's
sure, slow arrival to nowhere.
It is now one makes a show of praise

for the lilac that strains so hard to win
attention to its sweet inscrutability,
when one admires instead the lowly

gouge, adze, rasp, hammer—
fire-forged, blunt-syllabled things,
unthought-of until a need exists:

a groove chiseled to a fixed width,
a roof sloped just so. It is now
one knows what it is to envy

the rivet, wrench, vise—whatever
works unburdened by memory and sight,
while high above the damp fields

flocks of swallows roil and dip,
and streams churn, thick with leaping salmon,
and the bee advances on the rose.

# Mark Wunderlich

## THE BRUISE OF THIS | 059

The night I woke to find the sheets wet from you,
like a man cast up on the beach,
I hurried you off to the shower to cool you down,

dressed you, the garments strict and awkward in my hands,
and got you into a taxi to the hospital,
the driver eyeing us from his rearview mirror—

The blue tone of the paging bell,
the green smocks, metal beds,
plastic chairs linked

in a childhood diagram of infection,
and when they wheeled you by
there was a needle in your arm,

the bruise of this
already showing itself,
and rather than watch gloved doctors handle you

in their startling white coats and loose ties,
I took a seat outside and waited,
time yawning, thick and static—

and made clear to me in the bright light of speculation
was time's obstacle in the body,
and those things I could do that might cushion it.

# Catherine Bowman

## 1-800-HOT-RIBS | 060

My brother sent me ribs for my birthday.
He sent me two six-pound, heavily scented,
slow-smoked slabs, Federal Express,
in a customized cardboard box, no bigger
than a baby coffin or a bulrush ark.

Swaddled tight in sheaves of foam and dry ice,
those ribs rested in the hold of some jetliner
and were carried high, over the Yellowhammer State
and the Magnolia State and the Brown Thrasher State,
over Kentucky coffeetrees and Sitka spruce

and live oak and wild oak and lowland plains
and deep-water harbors, over catfish farms
and single-crib barns and Holiness sects
and strip malls and mill towns and lumber
towns and coal camps and chemical plants,

to my table on this island on a cold night
with no moon where I eat those ribs and am made
full from what must have been a young animal,
small-boned and tender, having just
the right ratio of meat to fat.

Tonight outside, men and women enrobed
in blankets fare forth from shipping crates.

A bloodhound lunges against its choke
to sniff the corpse of a big rat and heaps
of drippings and grounds that steam

outside the diner as an ashen woman deep
in a doorway presses a finger to her lips.
A matted teddy bear impaled on a spike
looms over a vacant lot where a line of men
wreathe in fellowship around a blazing garbage can.

Tonight in a dream they gather
all night to labor over the unadorned
beds they have dug into the ground and filled
with the hardwood coals that glow like remote stars.
Their faces molten and ignited in the damp,

they know to turn the meat infrequently,
they know to keep the flame slow and the fire
cool. From a vat of spirits subacid and brackish,
they know to baste only occasionally. So that
by sunrise vapor will continue to collect, as usual,

forming, as it should, three types of clouds,
that the rainfall from the clouds, it is certain,
will not exceed the capacity of the river,
that the river will still flow, as always,
sweet brother, on course.

## Aaron Fogel

Fellow compositors
and pressworkers!

I, Chief Printer
Frank Steinman,
having worked fifty-
seven years at my trade,
and served five years
as president
of the Holliston
Printer's Council,
being of sound mind
though near death,
leave this testimonial
concerning the nature
of printers' errors.

First: I hold that all books
and all printed
matter have
errors, obvious or no,
and that these are their
most significant moments,
not to be tampered with
by the vanity and folly

of ignorant, academic
textual editors.
Second: I hold that there are
three types of errors, in ascending
order of importance:
One: chance errors
of the printer's trembling hand
not to be corrected incautiously
by foolish professors
and other such rabble
because trembling is part
of divine creation itself.

Two: silent, cool sabotage
by the printer,
the manual laborer
whose protests
have at times taken this
historical form,
covert interferences
not to be corrected
censoriously by the hand
of the second and far
more ignorant saboteur,
the textual editor.

Three: errors
from the touch of God,
divine and often
obscure corrections
of whole books by
nearly unnoticed changes
of single letters
sometimes meaningful but
about which the less said
by preemptive commentary
the better.
Third: I hold that all three
sorts of error,
errors by chance,
errors by workers' protest,
and errors by
God's touch,
*are in practice the*
*same and indistinguishable.*

Therefore I,
Frank Steinman,
typographer
for thirty-seven years,
and cooperative Master

of the Holliston Guild
eight years,
being of sound mind and body
though near death
urge the abolition
of all editorial work
whatsoever
and manumission
from all textual editing
to leave what was
as it was, and
as it became,
except insofar as editing
is itself an error, and

therefore also divine.

## Nick Flynn

Children under, say, *ten*, shouldn't know
that the universe is ever-expanding,
inexorably pushing into the vacuum, galaxies

swallowed by galaxies, whole

solar systems collapsing, all of it
acted out in silence. At ten we are still learning

the rules of cartoon animation,

that if a man draws a door on a rock
only he can pass through it.
Anyone else who tries

will crash into the rock. Ten-year-olds
should stick with burning houses, car wrecks,
ships going down—earthbound, tangible

disasters, arenas

where they can be heroes. You can run
back into a burning house, sinking ships

have lifeboats, the trucks will come
with their ladders, if you jump

you will be saved. A child

places her hand on the roof of a schoolbus,
& drives across a city of sand. She knows

the exact spot it will skid, at which point
the bridge will give, who will swim to safety
& who will be pulled under by sharks. She will learn

that if a man runs off the edge of a cliff
he will not fall

until he notices his mistake.

## Bill Knott

I lay down in the empty street and parked
My feet against the gutter's curb while from
The building above a bunch of gawkers perched
Along its ledges urged me don't, don't jump.

*Daisy Fried*

Oh, she was sad, oh, she was sad.
She didn't mean to do it.

Certain thrills stay tucked in your limbs,
go no further than your fingers, move your legs through
their paces,
but no more. Certain thrills knock you flat
on your sheets on your bed in your room and you fade
and they fade. You falter and they're gone, gone, gone.
Certain thrills puff off you like smoke rings,
some like bell rings growing out, out, turning
brass, steel, gold, till the whole world's filled
with the gonging of your thrills.

But oh, she was sad, she was just sad, sad,
and she didn't mean to do it.

# David Berman

Walking through a field with my little brother Seth

I pointed to a place where kids had made angels in the
    snow.
For some reason, I told him that a troop of angels
had been shot and dissolved when they hit the ground.

He asked who had shot them and I said a farmer.


Then we were on the roof of the lake.
The ice looked like a photograph of water.

Why he asked. Why did he shoot them.

I didn't know where I was going with this.

They were on his property, I said.


When it's snowing, the outdoors seem like a room.

Today I traded hellos with my neighbor.
Our voices hung close in the new acoustics.
A room with the walls blasted to shreds and falling.

We returned to our shoveling, working side by side in
    silence.


But why were they on his property, he asked.

# Tom Andrews

Film Noir
Everyone on earth is asleep—except Robert Mitchum.

French Flick
The camera is an emptiness that longs to be a camera.

Historical Epic
Thousands of extras . . . reset their alarm clocks.

Stéphane Mallarmé Counts the Buttons on the Hangman's
    Vest
Mallarmé: Two, three . . . no . . . two . . . no . . . wait, two,
    three . . . one, two . . .

God, Guilt, and Death
This will not work on film.

The Needle
Medium shot of a camel squeezing through the eye of a
    needle.

# Hal Sirowitz

## I FINALLY MANAGED TO
## SPEAK TO HER | 067

She was sitting across from me
on the bus. I said, "The trees
look so much greener in this part
of the country. In New York City
everything looks so drab." She said,
"It looks the same to me. Show me
a tree that's different." "That one,"
I said. "Which one?" she said.
"It's too late," I said; "we already
passed it." "When you find another one,"
she said, "let me know." And then
she went back to reading her book.

# Karen Chase

## BEFORE SHE DIED | 068

When I look at the sky now, I look at it for you.
As if with enough attention, I could take it in for you.

With all the leaves gone almost from
the trees, I did not walk briskly through the field.

Late today with my dog Wool, I lay down in the upper field,
he panting and aged, me looking at the blue. Leaning

on him, I wondered how finite these lustered days seem
to you. A stand of hemlock across the lake catches

my eye. It will take a long time to know how it is
for you. Like a dog's lifetime—long—multiplied by sevens.

## Andrew Hudgins

My father cinched the rope,
a noose around my waist,
and lowered me into
the darkness. I could taste

my fear. It tasted first
of dark, then earth, then rot.
I swung and struck my head
and at that moment got

another then: then blood,
which spiked my mouth with iron.
Hand over hand, my father
dropped me from then to then:

then water. Then wet fur,
which I hugged to my chest.
I shouted. Daddy hauled
the wet rope. I gagged, and pressed

my neighbor's missing dog
against me. I held its death
and rose up to my father.
Then light. Then hands. Then breath.

# Paul Muldoon

## THE SONOGRAM | 070

Only a few weeks ago, the sonogram of Jean's womb
resembled nothing so much
as a satellite-map of Ireland:

now the image
is so well-defined we can make out not only a hand
but a thumb;

on the road to Spiddal, a woman hitching a ride;
a gladiator in his net, passing judgement on the crowd.

## Lisel Mueller

### LOVE LIKE SALT | 071

It lies in our hands in crystals
too intricate to decipher

It goes into the skillet
without being given a second thought

It spills on the floor so fine
we step all over it

We carry a pinch behind each eyeball

It breaks out on our foreheads

We store it inside our bodies
in secret wineskins

At supper, we pass it around the table
talking of holidays by the sea.

# Nicholas Christopher

## THROUGH THE WINDOW OF THE
## ALL-NIGHT RESTAURANT | 072

across from the gas station
a bus stopped every ten minutes
under the blue streetlight
and discharged a single passenger.
Never more than one.
A one-armed man with a cane.
A girl in red leather.
A security guard carrying his lunch box.
They stepped into the light,
looked left, then right, and disappeared.
Otherwise, the street was empty,
the wind off the river gusting paper and leaves.
Then the pay phone near the bus stop
started ringing; for five minutes it rang,
until another bus pulled in
and a couple stepped off,
their hats pulled down low
The man walked up the street,
but the woman hesitated,
then answered the phone and stood
frozen with the receiver to her ear.
The man came back for her,
but she waved him away

and at the same moment her hat blew off
and skidded down the street.
The man followed it, holding his own hat,
and the woman began talking into the phone.
And she kept talking,
the wind tossing her hair wildly,
and the man never returned
and no more buses came after that.

# David Wojahn

Smuggled human hair from Mexico
Falls radiant around the waxy *O*

Of her scream. Shades on, leather coat and pants, Yoko
On her knees—like the famous Kent State photo

Where the girl can't shriek her boyfriend alive, her arms
Windmilling Ohio sky.
                              A pump in John's chest heaves

To mimic death-throes. The blood is made of latex.
His glasses: broken on the plastic sidewalk.

A scowling David Chapman, his arms outstretched,
His pistol barrel spiraling fake smoke

In a siren's red wash, completes the composition,
And somewhere background music plays *Imagine*

Before the tableau darkens. We push a button
To renew the scream.
                              The chest starts up again.

# Lynne McMahon

## BARBIE'S FERRARI | 074

Nothing is quite alien or quite recognizable at this speed,
Though there is the suggestion of curve, a mutant
Curvature designed, I suppose, to soften or offset
The stiletto toes and karate arms that were too
Angular for her last car, a Corvette as knifed as Barbie
Herself, and not the bloodred of Italian Renaissance.
This is Attention. This is detail fitted to sheer
Velocity. For her knees, after all, are locked—
Once fitted into the driving pit, she can only accelerate
Into a future that becomes hauntingly like the past:
Nancy Drew in her yellow roadster, a convertible,
I always imagined, the means to an end
Almost criminal in its freedom, its motherlessness.
For Barbie, too, is innocent of parents, pressing
Her unloved breasts to the masculine wheel, gunning
The turn into the hallway and out over the maiming stairs,
Every jolt slamming her uterus into uselessness, sealed,
Sealed up and preserved, everything about her becoming
Pure Abstraction and the vehicle for Desire: to be Nancy,
To be Barbie, to feel the heaven of Imagination
Breathe its ether on your cheeks, rosying in the slipstream
As the speedster/roadster/Ferrari plummets over the rail
Into the ocean of waxed hardwood below. To crash and burn
And be retrieved. To unriddle the crime. To be
Barbie with a plot! That's the soulful beauty of it.

That's the dreaming child.
Not the dawn of Capital, or the factories of Hong Kong
Reversing the currency in Beijing. Not the ovarian
Moon in eclipse. Just the dreaming child, the orphan,
Turning in slow motion in the air above the bannister,
For whom ideas of gender and marketplace are nothings
Less than nothing. It's the car she was born for.
It's Barbie you mourn for.

# Paul Zimmer

They are so cowardly and stupid
Indians would not eat them
For fear of assuming their qualities.

The wild turkey always stays close
To home, flapping up into trees
If alarmed, then falling out again.
When shot it explodes like a balloon
Full of blood. It bathes by grinding
Itself in coarse dirt, is incapable
Of passion or anger, knows only
Vague innocence and extreme caution,
Walking around in underbrush
Like a cantilevered question mark,
Retreating at the least hint of danger.

I hope when the wild turkey
Dreams at night it flies high up
In gladness under vast islands
Of mute starlight, its silhouette
Vivid in the full moon, guided always
By radiant configurations high
Over chittering fields of corn
And the trivial fires of men,
Never to land again nor be regarded
As fearful, stupid, and unsure.

# Lisa Jarnot

Ye white antarctic birds of upper 57th street,
you gallery of white antarctic birds, you
street with white antarctic birds and
cabs and white antarctic birds you street,
ye and you the street and birds I walk upon
the galleries of streets and birds and longings,
you the birds antarctic of the conversations
and bank machines, you the atm of
longing, the longing for the atm machines,
you the lover of banks and me and birds
and others too and cabs, and you the cabs
and you the subtle longing birds and me,
and you the conversations yet antarctic, and
soup and teeming white antarctic birds and
you the books and phones and atms the bank
machines antarctic, and you the banks and
cabs, and him the one I love, and those who
love me not, and all antarctic longings, and
all the birds and cabs and also on the street
antarctic of this longing.

# Galway Kinnell

The bud
stands for all things,
even those things that don't flower,
for everything flowers, from within, of self-blessing;
though sometimes it is necessary
to reteach a thing its loveliness,
to put a hand on its brow
of the flower
and retell it in words and in touch
it is lovely
until it flowers again from within, of self-blessing;
as St. Francis
put his hand on the creased forehead
of the sow, and told her in words and in touch
blessings of earth on the sow, and the sow
began remembering all down her thick length,
from the earthen snout all the way
through the fodder and slops to the spiritual curl of
   the tail,
from the hard spininess spiked out from the spine
down through the great broken heart
to the blue milken dreaminess spurting and shuddering
from the fourteen teats into the fourteen mouths sucking
   and blowing beneath them:
the long, perfect loveliness of sow.

# Wesley McNair

The chickens cannot
find their heads
though they search for them,
falling in the grass.

And the great bulls
remain on their knees,
unable to remember
how to stand.

The goats cannot find their voices.
They run quickly
on their sides,
watching the sky.

# Robert Hedin

Of all the people in the mornings at the mall,
It's the old liberators I like best,
Those veterans of the Bulge, Anzio, or Monte Cassino
I see lost in Automotive or back in Home Repair,
Bored among the paints and power tools.
Or the *really* old ones, the ones who are going fast,
Who keep dozing off in the little orchards
Of shade under the distant skylights.
All around, from one bright rack to another,
Their wives stride big as generals,
Their handbags bulging like ripe fruit.
They are almost all gone now,
And with them they are taking the flak
And fire storms, the names of the old bombing runs.
Each day a little more of their memory goes out,
Darkens the way a house darkens,
Its rooms quietly filling with evening,
Until nothing but the wind lifts the lace curtains,
The wind bearing through the empty rooms
The rich far off scent of gardens
Where just now, this morning,
Light is falling on the wild philodendrons.

## Robert Hershon

### SENTIMENTAL MOMENT OR WHY DID THE BAGUETTE CROSS THE ROAD? | 080

Don't fill up on bread
I say absent-mindedly
The servings here are huge

My son, whose hair may be
receding a bit, says
Did you really just
say that to me?

What he doesn't know
is that when we're walking
together, when we get
to the curb
I sometimes start to reach
for his hand

# Tony Hoagland

Maxine, back from a weekend with her boyfriend,
smiles like a big cat and says
that she's a conjugated verb.
She's been doing the direct object
with a second person pronoun named Phil,
and when she walks into the room,
everybody turns:

some kind of light is coming from her head.
Even the geraniums look curious,
and the bees, if they were here, would buzz
suspiciously around her hair, looking
for the door in her corona.
We're all attracted to the perfume
of fermenting joy,

we've all tried to start a fire,
and one day maybe it will blaze up on its own.
In the meantime, she is the one today among us
most able to bear the idea of her own beauty,
and when we see it, what we do is natural:
we take our burned hands
out of our pockets,
and clap.

# Thomas Lux

## PLAGUE VICTIMS CATAPULTED OVER
## WALLS INTO BESIEGED CITY | 082

Early germ
warfare. The dead
hurled this way turn like wheels
in the sky. Look: there goes
Larry the Shoemaker, barefoot, over the wall,
and Mary Sausage Stuffer, see how she flies,
and the Hatter twins, both at once, soar
over the parapet, little Tommy's elbow bent
as if in a salute,
and his sister, Mathilde, she follows him,
arms outstretched, through the air,
just as she did on earth.

# Judith Kerman

wet-ash light
blows across the road
I'm driving with my foot to the floor
sixty miles over flat midwestern highway
driving to hear poetry
the sky ready
to boil over, a lid clamped on
the pressure drops
flattens the landscape further
I watch the horizon for state troopers
think of the wind:
one hundred miles to the west it has
sliced the top off a hospital
smashed two miles of Kalamazoo
nothing anyone will read tonight
is wild enough

# George Green

Without you I am like the Portuguese in Mergui
who have forgotten their language
but still go to church,
unlike their neighbors, the Salon pirates,
who live near the mudbanks
trading pearls for opium.

Without you I am a geopolitical feature
like Lot's wife, who only turned her head
like a doe in the forest
to watch the flaming city
crackle and poof.

Without you I must wait in this neglected park alone,
and though I might need a shoeshine
my bright red sport jacket
lends me the prominence of a woodpecker
and the authority of a rooster.

Without you I have brung a cupcake
for the birthday of Chester Nimitz,
who, reared among the dry hills of Texas,
far from any sea shore,

rose to command the mightiest armada
in the history of the world.

And am I not myself an admiral of the clouds?
As such I now command you to come home.

# William Matthews

I like divorce. I love to compose
letters of resignation; now and then
I send one in and leave in a lemon-
hued Huff or a Snit with four on the floor.
Do you like the scent of a hollyhock?
To each his own. I love a burning bridge.

I like to watch the small boat go over
the falls—it swirls in a circle
like a dog coiling for sleep, and its frail bow
pokes blindly out over the falls' lip
a little and a little more and then
too much, and then the boat's nose dives and butt

flips up so that the boat points doomily
down and the screams of the soon-to-be-dead
last longer by echo than the screamers do.
Let's go to the videotape, the news-
caster intones, and the control room does,
and the boat explodes again and again.

# Robert Phillips

## THE PANIC BIRD | 086

just flew inside my chest. Some
days it lights inside my brain,
but today it's in my bonehouse,
rattling ribs like a birdcage.

If I saw it coming, I'd fend it
off with machete or baseball bat.
Or grab its scrawny hackled neck,
wring it like a wet dishrag.

But it approaches from behind.
Too late I sense it at my back—
carrion, garbage, excrement.
Once inside me it preens, roosts,

vulture on a public utility pole.
Next it flaps, it cries, it glares,
it rages, it struts, it thrusts
its clacking beak into my liver,

my guts, my heart, rips off strips.
I fill with black blood, black bile.
This may last minutes or days.
Then it lifts sickle-shaped wings,

rises, is gone, leaving a residue—
foul breath, droppings, molted midnight
feathers. And life continues.
And then I'm prey to panic again.

# Benjamin Saltman

Do you seriously want peace or a good meal
in a restaurant opening onto a garden?
A garden with lights strung in a tree
and raccoons visiting every night,
cleverness in little hands? The raccoons
ignore the lights and the people watching.
The light gleaming along wet telephone
wires and collecting on the white
stone bench.

          Inside the restaurant I think
of reading my book or tarring my roof
knowing I can still do one but not the other.
For five years I've been waiting to die
and trying to think of something significant.
I wait for a key to slam into a door,
and I sit straight with folded hands.
At least I know how to imitate peace.

Earlier when I saw a man in a black coat
standing in the cold with his children
it was as if they had been standing forever
on a little island. How could they not be
significant? The man would touch his children
on the shoulders at times as if to say
that people would not be this way forever,
that he would forget peace for a meal.

# Jane Kenyon

I got out of bed
on two strong legs.
It might have been
otherwise. I ate
cereal, sweet
milk, ripe, flawless
peach. It might
have been otherwise.
I took the dog uphill
to the birch wood.
All morning I did
the work I love.

At noon I lay down
with my mate. It might
have been otherwise.
We ate dinner together
at a table with silver
candlesticks. It might
have been otherwise.
I slept in a bed
in a room with paintings
on the walls, and
planned another day
just like this day.
But one day, I know,
it will be otherwise.

# Taslima Nasrin

My life,
like a sandbar, has been taken over by a monster of a man.
He wants my body under his control
so that if he wishes he can spit in my face,
    slap me on the cheek
and pinch my rear.
So that if he wishes he can rob me of my clothes
and take the naked beauty in his grip.
So that if he wishes he can pull out my eyes,
so that if he wishes he can chain my feet,
if he wishes, he can, with no qualms whatsoever,
    use a whip on me,
if he wishes he can chop off my hands, my fingers.
If he wishes he can sprinkle salt in the open wound,
he can throw ground-up black pepper in my eyes.
So that if he wishes he can slash my thigh with a dagger,
so that if he wishes he can string me up and hang me.

He wanted my heart under his control
so that I would love him:
in my lonely house at night,
sleepless, full of anxiety,
clutching at the window grille,
    I would wait for him and sob.

My tears rolling down, I would bake homemade bread;
so that I would drink, as if they were ambrosia,
the filthy liquids of his polygynous body.
So that, loving him, I would melt like wax,
not turning my eyes toward any other man,
I would give proof of my chastity all my life.
So that, loving him
on some moonlit night I would commit suicide
      in a fit of ecstasy.

## Sherman Alexie

### AT NAVAJO MONUMENT VALLEY TRIBAL SCHOOL (FROM THE PHOTOGRAPH BY SKEET MCAULEY) | 090

the football field rises
to meet the mesa. Indian boys
gallop across the grass, against

the beginning of their body.
On those Saturday afternoons,
unbroken horses gather to watch

their sons growing larger
in the small parts of the world.
Everyone is the quarterback.

There is no thin man in a big hat
writing down all the names
in two columns: winners and losers.

This is the eternal football game,
Indians versus Indians. All the Skins
in the wooden bleachers fancydancing,

stomping red dust straight down
into nothing. Before the game is over,
the eighth-grade girls' track team

comes running, circling the field,
their thin and brown legs echoing
wild horses, wild horses, wild horses.

## D. C. Berry

Laertes has groupies, proof he has taste,
has cool. Wears skate-board clothes: elephant pants,
the crotch snagging his knees, tent-size tee-shirt.
He wants the play staged at a roller rink:
him, Fortinbras, and me wearing in-lines,
the rest in quads. And instead of a duel,
we throw ourselves a roller-derby brawl.
Why not? Do something with a little class
to offset the end's cartoon slaughter house.

## Forrest Hamer

### LESSON | 092

It was 1963 or 4, summer,
and my father was driving our family
from Ft. Hood to North Carolina in our 56 Buick.
We'd been hearing about Klan attacks, and we knew

Mississippi to be more dangerous than usual.
Dark lay hanging from the trees the way moss did,
and when it moaned light against the windows
that night, my father pulled off the road to sleep.

    Noises
that usually woke me from rest afraid of monsters
kept my father awake that night, too,
and I lay in the quiet noticing him listen, learning
that he might not be able always to protect us

from everything and the creatures besides;
perhaps not even from the fury suddenly loud
through my body about his trip from Texas
to settle us home before he would go away

to a place no place in the world
he named Viet Nam. A boy needs a father
with him, I kept thinking, fixed against noise
from the dark.

# Louis Jenkins

I take the snap from the center, fake to the right, fade
back . . .
I've got protection. I've got a receiver open downfield . . .
What the hell is this? This isn't a football, it's a shoe,
a man's
brown leather oxford. A cousin to a football maybe, the
same
skin, but not the same, a thing made for the earth, not the
air.
I realize that this is a world where anything is possible
and I
understand, also, that one often has to make do with what
one
has. I have eaten pancakes, for instance, with that clear
corn
syrup on them because there was no maple syrup and they
weren't very good. Well, anyway, this is different. (My man
downfield is waving his arms.) One has certain
responsibilities,
one has to make choices. This isn't right and I'm not going
to throw it.

# Jane Yolen

## FAT IS NOT A FAIRY TALE | 094

I am thinking of a fairy tale,
Cinder Elephant,
Sleeping Tubby,
Snow Weight,
where the princess is not
anorexic, wasp-waisted;
flinging herself down the stairs.

I am thinking of a fairy tale,
Hansel and Great,
Repoundsel,
Bounty and the Beast,
where the beauty
has a pillowed breast,
and fingers plump as sausage.

I am thinking of a fairy tale
that is not yet written,
for a teller not yet born,
for a listener not yet conceived,
for a world not yet won,
where everything round is good:
the sun, wheels, cookies, and the princess.

# Frances Mayes

Cat stands at the fridge,
Cries loudly for milk.
But I've filled her bowl.
Wild cat, I say, Sister,
Look, you *have* milk.
I clink my fingernail
Against the rim. *Milk.*
With *down* and *liver,*
A word I know she hears.
Her sad miaow. She runs
To me. She dips
In her whiskers but
Doesn't drink. As sometimes
I want the light on
When it is on. Or when
I saw the woman walking
toward my house and
I thought *there's Frances.*
Then looked in the car mirror
To be sure. She stalks
The room. She wants. Milk
Beyond milk. World beyond
This one, she cries.

# David Ignatow

## THE BAGEL | 096

I stopped to pick up the bagel
rolling away in the wind,
annoyed with myself
for having dropped it
as if it were a portent.
Faster and faster it rolled,
with me running after it
bent low, gritting my teeth,
and I found myself doubled over
and rolling down the street
head over heels, one complete somersault
after another like a bagel
and strangely happy with myself.

# Adam Zagajewski

The rivers of this country are sweet
as a troubadour's song,
the heavy sun wanders westward
on yellow circus wagons.
Little village churches
hold a fabric of silence so fine
and old that even a breath
could tear it.
I love to swim in the sea, which keeps
talking to itself
in the monotone of a vagabond
who no longer recalls
exactly how long he's been on the road.
Swimming is like prayer:
palms join and part,
join and part,
almost without end.

# Jenny Factor

In the never truly ever
truly dark dark night, ever
blinds-zipped, slat-cut,
dark-parked light,
you (late) touch my toes
with your broad flat own
horny-nailed cold toes.
Clock-tock, wake-shock.

In the ever truly never
truly long long night, our
little snoring-snarling
wild-child mild-child
starling-darling wakes every
two, three (you-sleep) hours,
in the never truly ever
truly lawn brawn fawn dawn.

## Luisa Villani

*I hang the window inside out*
          *like a shirt drying in a breeze*
*and the arms that are missing come to me*
          Yes, it's a song, one I don't quite comprehend
although I do understand the laundry.
          White ash and rain water, a method
my aunt taught me, but I'll never know
          how she learned it in Brooklyn. Her mind
has gone to seed, blown by a stroke,
          and that dandelion puff called memory
has flown far from her eyes. Some things remain.
          Procedures. Methods. If you burn
a fire all day, feeding it snapped
          branches and newspapers—
the faces pressed against the print
          fading into flames—you end up
with a barrel of white ash. If
          you take that same barrel and fill it
with rain, let it sit for a day,
          you will have water
that can bring brightness to anything.
          If you take that water,
and in it soak your husband's shirts,
          he'll pause at dawn when he puts one on,

its softness like a haunting afterthought.
　　　And if he works all day in the *selva*,
he'll divine his way home
　　　　　in shirtsleeves aglow with torchlight.

# Carol Ann Duffy

Ice in the trees.
Three Queens at the Palace gates,
dressed in furs, accented;
their several sweating, panting beasts,
laden for a long, hard trek,
following the guide and boy to the stables;
courteous, confident; oh, and with gifts
for the King and Queen of here—Herod, me—
in exchange for sunken baths, curtained beds,
fruit, the best of meat and wine,
dancers, music, talk—
as it turned out to be,
with everyone fast asleep, save me,
those vivid three—
till bitter dawn.

They were wise. Older than I.
They knew what they knew.
Once drunken Herod's head went back,
they asked to see her,
fast asleep in her crib,
my little child.
Silver and gold,
the loose change of herself,
glowed in the soft bowl of her face.

*Grace*, said the tallest Queen.
*Strength*, said the Queen with the hennaed hands.
The black Queen
made a tiny starfish of my daughter's fist,
said *Happiness*; then stared at me,
Queen to Queen, with insolent lust.
*Watch*, they said, *for a star in the East—*
*a new star*
*pierced through the night like a nail.*
*It means he's here, alive, new-born.*
Who? *Him. The Husband. Hero. Hunk.*
*The Boy Next Door. The Paramour. The* Je t'adore.
*The Marrying Kind. Adulterer. Bigamist.*
*The Wolf. The Rip. The Rake. The Rat.*
*The Heartbreaker. The Ladykiller. Mr. Right.*

My baby stirred,
suckled the empty air for milk,
till I knelt
and the black Queen scooped out my breast,
the left, guiding it down
to the infant's mouth.
*No man*, I swore,
*will make her shed one tear.*
A peacock screamed outside.

Afterwards, it seemed like a dream.
The pungent camels
kneeling in the snow,
the guide's rough shout
as he clapped his leather gloves,
hawked, spat, snatched
the smoky jug of mead
from the chittering maid—
she was twelve, thirteen.
I watched each turbaned Queen
rise like a god on the back of her beast.
And splayed that night
below Herod's fusty bulk,
I saw the fierce eyes of the black Queen
flash again, felt her urgent warnings scald
my ear. *Watch for a star, a star.*
*It means he's here . . .*

Some swaggering lad to break her heart,
some wincing Prince to take her name away
and give a ring, a nothing, nowt in gold.
I sent for the Chief of Staff,
a mountain man
with a red scar, like a tick
to the mean stare of his eye.

*Take men and horses,*
*knives, swords, cutlasses.*
*Ride East from here*
*and kill each mother's son.*
*Do it. Spare not one.*

# Mary Jo Salter

My husband has a crush on Myrna Loy,
and likes to rent her movies, for a treat.
It makes some evenings harder to enjoy.

The list of actresses who might employ
him as their slave is too long to repeat.
(My husband has a crush on Myrna Loy,

Carole Lombard, Paulette Goddard, coy
Jean Arthur with that voice as dry as wheat . . .)
It makes some evenings harder to enjoy.

Does he confess all this just to annoy
a loyal spouse? I know I can't compete.
My husband has a crush on Myrna Loy.

And can't a woman have her dreamboats? Boy,
I wouldn't say my life is incomplete,
but some evening I could certainly enjoy

two hours with Cary Grant as *my* own toy.
I guess, though, we were destined not to meet.
My husband has a crush on Myrna Loy,
which makes some evenings harder to enjoy.

# Elton Glaser

## SMOKING | 102

I like the cool and heft of it, dull metal on the palm,
And the click, the hiss, the spark fuming into flame,
Boldface of fire, the rage and sway of it, raw blue at the
    base
And a slope of gold, a touch to the packed tobacco, the tip
Turned red as a warning light, blown brighter by the
    breath,
The pull and the pump of it, and the paper's white
Smoothed now to ash as the smoke draws back, drawn down
To the black crust of lungs, tar and poisons in the pink,
And the blood sorting it out, veins tight and the heart
    slow,
The push and wheeze of it, a sweep of plumes in the air
Like a shako of horses dragging a hearse through the late
    centennium,
London, at the end of December, in the dark and fog.

# B. H. Fairchild

The heavy bodies lunge, the broken language
of fake and drive, glamorous jump shot
slowed to a stutter. Their gestures, in love
again with the pure geometry of curves,

rise toward the ball, falter, and fall away.
On the boards their hands and fingertips
tremble in tense little prayers of reach
and balance. Then, the grind of bone

and socket, the caught breath, the sigh,
the grunt of the body laboring to give
birth to itself. In their toiling and grand
sweeps, I wonder, do they still make love

to their wives, kissing the undersides
of their wrists, dancing the old soft-shoe
of desire? And on the long walk home
from the VFW, do they still sing

to the drunken moon? Stands full, clock
moving, the one in army fatigues
and houseshoes says to himself, *pick and roll*,
and the phrase sounds musical as ever,

radio crooning songs of love after the game,
the girl leaning back in the Chevy's front seat
as her raven hair flames in the shuddering
light of the outdoor movie, and now he drives,

gliding toward the net. A glass wand
of autumn light breaks over the backboard.
Boys rise up in old men, wings begin to sprout
at their backs. The ball turns in the darkening air.

## Robert Bly

When we stride or stroll across the frozen lake,
We place our feet where they have never been.
We walk upon the unwalked. But we are uneasy.
Who is down there but our old teachers?

Water that once could take no human weight—
We were students then—holds up our feet,
And goes on ahead of us for a mile.
Beneath us the teachers, and around us the stillness.

# David Lehman

It's my birtday I've got an empty
stomach and the desire to be
lazy in the hammock and maybe
go for a cool swim on a hot day
with the trombone in Sinatra's
"I've Got You Under My Skin"
in my head and then to break for
lunch a corned-beef sandwich and Pepsi
with plenty of ice cubes unlike France
where they put one measly ice cube
in your expensive Coke and when
you ask for more they argue with
you they say this way you get more
Coke for the money showing they
completely misunderstand the nature of
American soft drinks which are an
excuse for ice cubes still I wouldn't
mind being there for a couple of
days Philip Larkin's attitude
toward China comes to mind when
asked if he'd like to go there he said
yes if he could return the same day

# David Clewell

The tofu that's shown up overnight in this house is
    frightening
proof of the Law of Conservation: matter that simply
    cannot be
created or destroyed. Matter older than Newton,
who knew better than to taste it. Older than Lao-tzu,
who thought about it but finally chose harmonious non-
    interference.
I'd like to be philosophical too, see it as some kind of pale
inscrutable wisdom among the hot dogs, the cold chicken,
the leftover deviled eggs, but I'm talking curdled
soybean milk. And I don't have that kind of energy.

I'd rather not be part of the precariously metaphorical
wedding of modern physics and the ancient Eastern
    mysteries.
But still: whoever stashed the tofu in my Frigidaire
had better come back for it soon. I'm not Einstein
but I'm smart enough to know a bad idea when I see it
taking up space, biding its time.
Like so much that demands our imperfect attention
amid the particle roar of the world: going nowhere, fast.

# Joe Wenderoth

## MY LIFE | 107

*after Henri Michaux*

Somehow it got into my room.
I found it, and it was, naturally, trapped.
It was nothing more than a frightened animal.
Since then I raised it up.
I kept it for myself, kept it in my room,
kept it for its own good.
I named the animal, My Life.
I found food for it and fed it with my bare hands.
I let it into my bed, let it breathe in my sleep.
And the animal, in my love, my constant care,
grew up to be strong, and capable of many clever tricks.
One day, quite recently,
I was running my hand over the animal's side
and I came to understand
that it could very easily kill me.
I realized, further, that it would kill me.
This is why it exists, why I raised it.
Since then I have not known what to do.
I stopped feeding it,
only to find that its growth
has nothing to do with food.
I stopped cleaning it
and found that it cleans itself.

I stopped singing it to sleep
and found that it falls asleep faster without my song.
I don't know what to do.
I no longer make My Life do tricks.
I leave the animal alone
and, for now, it leaves me alone, too.
I have nothing to say, nothing to do.
Between My Life and me,
a silence is coming.
Together, we will not get through this.

# Edward Nobles

## NUCLEAR WINTER | 108

When the sky fell, the earth turned blue.
The trees, the tenements, the cars and buses
soaked up the sky and changed from outside in, in color,
to blue. The children ran frantically in adult directions.
    My wife,
dressed fashionably in blue, took my hand and, with sadness
in her deep blue eyes, led me behind the house, down the
    long incline, and into
the woods. We waded in blue snow through blue trees.
An iridescent crow, blue, flew from a branch, and a fox
lay in our tracks, oblivious to our passing. He licked his
    blue fur
with melancholic eyes. The years pass very quickly with
    this earth.
In that time, we had two children, the son and daughter
we always dreamt of, and they knelt above us, like two
    granite stones,
ghostly figures praying, for the love of God, for what he
    had become:
a family moved by that one clear color, blue, beneath the
    blue snow.

# J. Allyn Rosser

Ignore that last one I sent you.
I'd really rather you didn't
try to find me.

Everything human is perfect here, round,
worn smooth. These green bottles
and the bones beside them.

They clink and shift in the wind.
I take in lame snakes.
Sometimes I sing

and the birds sit up on their branches.
Time is the boomerang of sun.
At night the dark shapes

of island surround me; I remember myself
stupid among you, freeing prisoners
in love with their chains,

always taking, as was the custom, parts
for the whole—the body's cavities for what
they wanted: pupils

for the black opacities they saw through.
The mouth
for what it watered to surround.

## Robin Robertson

I have swum too far
out of my depth
and the sun has gone;

the hung weight of my legs
a plumb-line,
my fingers raw, my arms lead;

the currents pull like weed
and I am very tired
and cold, and moving out to sea.

The beach is still bright.
The children I never had
run to the edge

and back to their beautiful mother
who smiles at them, looks up
from her magazine, and waves.

# Charles Bukowski

NO. 6 | 111

I'll settle for the 6 horse
on a rainy afternoon
a paper cup of coffee
in my hand
a little way to go,
the wind twirling out
small wrens from
the upper grandstand roof,
the jocks coming out
for a middle race
silent
and the easy rain making
everything
at once
almost alike,
the horses at peace with
each other
before the drunken war
and I am under the grandstand
feeling for
cigarettes
settling for coffee,
then the horses walk by
taking their little men
away—

it is funereal and graceful
and glad
like the opening
of flowers.

# David Lee

The worse goddam job of all
sez John pushing a thick slat
in front of the posts
behind the sow in the loading chute
so when she balked and backed up
she couldn't turn and get away
I never seen a sow or a hog load easy
some boars will
mebbe it's because they got balls
or something I don't know
but I seen them do it
that Brown feller the FFA
he's got this boar he just opens the trailer door
he comes and gets in
course he mebbe knows what
he's being loaded up for

it was this Ivie boy back home
the best I ever seen for loading
he wasn't scared of nothing
he'd get right in and shove them up
he put sixteen top hogs
in the back of a Studebaker pickup
by hisself I seen it

when he was a boy he opened up
the tank on the tractor
smelling gas
made his brains go soft they sed
he failed fifth grade
but it wasn't his fault
he could load up hogs

I always had to at home
cause I was the youngest
I sed then it was two things
I wouldn't do when I grown up
warsh no dishes or load up hogs
by god they can set in the sink
a month before I'll warsh them
a man's got to have a principle
he can live by is what I say
now you grab her ears and pull
I'll push from back here
we'll get that sonofabitch in the truck.

## Naomi Shihab Nye

There is no stray bullet, sirs.

No bullet like a worried cat
crouching under a bush,
no half-hairless puppy bullet
dodging midnight streets.
The bullet could not be a pecan
plunking the tin roof,
not hardly, no fluff of pollen
on October's breath,
no humble pebble in the street.

So don't gentle it, please.

We live among stray thoughts,
tasks abandoned midstream.
Our fickle hearts are fat
with stray devotions, we feel at home
among bits and pieces,
all the wandering ways of words.

But this bullet had no innocence, did not
wish anyone well, you can't tell us otherwise
by naming it mildly, this bullet was never the friend
of life, should not be granted immunity

by soft saying—friendly fire, straying death-eye,
why have we given the wrong weight to what we do?

Mohammed, Mohammed, deserves the truth.

This bullet had no secret happy hopes,
it was not singing to itself with eyes closed under the
    bridge
like the exiled lady in her precious faded hat.

# Katha Pollitt

Coffee and cigarettes in a clean cafe,
forsythia lit like a damp match against
a thundery sky drunk on its own ozone,

the laundry cool and crisp and folded away
again in the lavender closet—too late to find
comfort enough in such small daily moments

of beauty, renewal, calm, too late to imagine
people would rather be happy than suffering
and inflicting suffering. We're near the end,

but O before the end, as the sparrows wing
each night to their secret nests in the elm's green dome
O let the last bus bring

love to lover, let the starveling
dog turn the corner and lope suddenly
miraculously, down its own street, home.

# Lucia Perillo

Back then it seemed that wherever a girl took off her
      clothes the police would find her—
in the backs of cars or beside the dark night ponds,
      opening like a green leaf across
some boy's knees, the skin so white and taut beneath the
      moor, it was almost too terrible,
too beautiful to look at, a tinderbox, though she did not
      know. But the men who came
beating the night rushes with their flashlights and
      thighs—they knew. About Helen,
about how a body could cause the fall of Troy and the
      death of a perfectly good king.
So they read the boy his rights and shoved him spread-
      legged against the car
while the girl hopped barefoot on the asphalt, cloaked in
      a wool rescue blanket.
Or sometimes girls fled so their fathers wouldn't hit
      them, their white legs flashing as they ran.
And the boys were handcuffed just until their wrists had
      welts and let off half a block from home.

God for how many years did I believe there were truly
      laws against such things,
laws of adulthood: no yelling out of cars in traffic tunnels,
      no walking without shoes,

no singing any foolish songs in public places. Or else they
    could lock you in jail
or, as good as condemning you to death, tell both your
    lower- and upper-case Catholic fathers.
And out of all these crimes, unveiling the body was of
    course the worst, as though something
about the skin's phosphorescence, its surface as velvet as
    a deer's new horn,
could drive not only men but civilization mad, could lead
    us to unspeakable cruelties.
There were elders who from experience understood these
    things much better than we.
And it's true: remembering I had that kind of skin does
    drive me half-crazy with loss.
Skin like the spathe of a broad white lily on the first
    morning it unfurls.

## Joseph Millar

All morning in the February light
he has been mending cable,
splicing the pairs of wires together
according to their colors,
white-blue to white-blue
violet-slate to violet-slate,
in the warehouse attic by the river.

When he is finished
the messages will flow along the line:
*thank you for the gift,*
*please come to the baptism,*
*the bill is now past due:*
voices that flicker and gleam back and forth
across the tracer-colored wires.

We live so much of our lives
without telling anyone,
going out before dawn,
working all day by ourselves,
shaking our heads in silence
at the news on the radio.
He thinks of the many signals
flying in the air around him,

the syllables fluttering,
saying *please love me*,
from continent to continent
over the curve of the earth.

## Marc Petersen

If my wife were to have an affair,
I would walk to my toolbox in the garage,
Take from it my 12" flathead screwdriver
And my hickory-handle hammer,
The one that helped me build three redwood fences,
And I would hammer out the pins
In all the door hinges in the house,
And I would pull off all the doors
And I would stack them in the backyard.
And I would empty all the sheets from the linen closet,
And especially the flannels we have slept between for
     nineteen winters;
And I would empty all the towels, too,
The big heavy white towels she bought on Saturdays at
     Target,
And the red bath towels we got for our wedding,
And which we have never used;
And I would unroll the aluminum foil from its box,
And carry all the pots and pans from the cupboards to the
     backyard,
And lay this one long sheet of aluminum foil over all our
     pots and pans;
And I would dump all the silverware from the drawer
Onto the driveway; and I would push my motorcycle over
And let all its gas leak out,

And I would leave my Jeep running at the curb
Until its tank was empty or its motor blew up,
And I would turn the TV up full-blast and open all the
    windows;
And I would turn the stereo up full-blast,
With Beethoven's Ninth Symphony on it,
Schiller's "Ode to Joy," really blasting;
And I would strip our bed;
And I would lie on our stripped bed;
And I would see our maple budding out the window.
I would see our maple budding out our window,
The hummingbird feeder hanging from its lowest bough.
And my cat would jump up to see what was the matter
    with me.
And I would tell her. Of course, I would tell her.
From her, I hold nothing back.

# Kate Knapp Johnson

## THE MEADOW | 118

Half the day lost, staring
at this window. I wanted to know
just one true thing

about the soul, but I left thinking
for thought, and now—
two inches of snow have fallen

over the meadow. Where did I go,
how long was I out looking
for you?, who would never leave me,
my withness, my here.

# Christina Pugh

Closer to a bell than a bird,
that clapper ringing
the clear name
of its inventor:

by turns louder
and quieter than a clock,
its numbered face
was more literate,

triplets of alphabet
like grace notes
above each digit.

And when you dialed,
each number was a shallow hole
your finger dragged
to the silver
comma-boundary,

then the sound of the hole
traveling back
to its proper place
on the circle.

You had to wait for its return.
You had to wait.
Even if you were angry
and your finger flew,

you had to await
the round trip
of seven holes
before you could speak.

The rotary was wired for lag,
for the afterthought.

Before the touch-tone,
before the speed-dial,
before the primal grip
of the cellular,

they built glass houses
around telephones:
glass houses in parking lots,
by the roadside,
on sidewalks.

When you stepped in
and closed the door,
transparency hugged you,
and you could almost see

your own lips move,
the dumb-show
of your new secrecy.

Why did no one think
to conserve the peal?

Just try once
to sing it to yourself:
it's gone,

like the sound of breath
if your body left.

# Mark Halliday

I saw you going into Sax's Steak Sandwiches
but what were you thinking?
It was a hot day, the downtown traffic
smashed itself right thru, right thru.
People wore their primary colors and
touched the doors and parking meters
and bottles and quarters and steering wheels
and the hold-on bars in bouncing busses
with tough hands, tools made of tough skin.
The sun was some ten degrees hotter than
anybody expected, this being not yet summer,
people folded their jackets and went to deal.
You must have been dealing too,
but what were you dealing with?
You came out of Sax's Steak Sandwiches
with a large Coke to go,
straw stuck thru plastic lid,
but what were you contemplating?
There was sweat in all armpits,
three ten-year-old boys had a hardball,
one of them shouted "Up your ass"
and laughed. Fifteen blocks away
an enormous insurance building glittered
with its violent impregnability in the hot sky.
It was real, as real as the hot yellow gas truck,
which was as real as the spice in Sax's chili,
and so were you no doubt but

what was your real point?
I mean what did you add up to?

You caught the Dudley bus
and sat next to a blind young man
whose fingers flickered every minute or so
in something like a diffident farewell to
someone important who might not return
for a long time. Staring
at the fingernails of the rider across from you,
you tapped your foot to a song called "Staying Alive"
from a black girl's huge radio—
and you may even have hummed along
while sucking ice from your tall cup—
however, the song's meaning for you
is not apparent;
                     and I don't know
why you got off where you did,
chucking your drained cup in a dumpster,
rolling up your sleeves as you passed the Purity Supreme . . .
I know exactly *where* you got off
and how hot the air was


but damn you! What were you *thinking*?
I've tried, I've tried to figure it
but it comes out different each time and
I can't be bothered—really,
if you have some hang-up about Being Mysterious
it's not my problem. So unless
you're willing to give me a clue—
just the general area, the basic subject,
something to get started is all,
you don't have to fork over your whole self—
but if it's just going to be trivia,
your shoes, your Coke, your moving lips,
then forget it—I'm serious—
just forget the whole thing.

## Diane Wakoski

### BLACK LEATHER BECAUSE
### BUMBLEBEES LOOK LIKE IT | 121

when the bumblebees ride their black motorcycles down
    to the
country to watch death swimming in the river, nude,
enjoying the summer, and me, gathering mushrooms in
    the shade
nearby,
everything is quiet and peaceful.
Death and I get along because we are not too personal.
And my life is like Chinese to him; he doesn't read it or
    understand.
But his black clothes and leather cap
thrown on the bank carelessly
remind me of my children, like hundreds of bee carcasses,
    tossed
                   together
and dead from a storm that wrecked the hive.
Watch him,
death,
climb out of the river, without his clothes.
Isn't he beautiful? A man built to swim and ride.
Shall we swim together, Mr. Big Beautiful, and Black Death?
        Push over the rocks,
           gather watercress, and smile at the fish?
Isn't it nice in the country, Mr. Death?

If I put a frame around your clothes, lying on the bank,
so that just in the corner of the picture, we might see one
of your bare feet climbing out of the water—
death's foot,
and the bees nearby, and me lying nude on the bank
    while the bees
ride by—
what would you think of that, Mr. Death?
Would you still think my name Chinese?
And would we still get along?
Oh, Mr. Death, I've seen you so many times.
How is it we meet so often, yet never speak?

# Sharon Bryan

Nothing matters
to the dead,
that's what's so hard

for the rest of us
to take in—
their complete indifference

to our enticements,
our attempts to get in touch—
they aren't observing us

from a discreet distance,
they aren't listening
to a word we say—

you *know* that,
but you don't believe it,
even deep in a cave

you don't believe
in total darkness,
you keep waiting

for your eyes to adjust
and reveal your hand
in front of your face—

so how long a silence
will it take to convince us
that we're the ones

who no longer exist,
as far as X is concerned,
and Y, that they've forgotten

every little thing
they knew about us,
what we told them

and what we didn't
have to, even our names
mean nothing to them

now—our throats ache
with all we might have said
the next time we saw them.

# Dana Gioia

## ALLEY CAT LOVE SONG | 123

Come into the garden, Fred,
For the neighborhood tabby is gone.
Come into the garden, Fred.
I have nothing but my flea collar on,
And the scent of catnip has gone to my head.
I'll wait by the screen door till dawn.

The fireflies court in the sweetgum tree.
The nightjar calls from the pine,
And she seems to say in her rhapsody,
"Oh, mustard-brown Fred, be mine!"
The full moon lights my whiskers afire,
And the fur goes erect on my spine.

I hear the frogs in the muddy lake
Croaking from shore to shore.
They've one swift season to soothe their ache.
In autumn they sing no more.
So ignore me now, and you'll hear my meow
As I scratch all night at the door.

# Wesley McNair

Goodbye to the old life,
to the sadness of rooms
where my family slept as I sat

late at night on my
island of light among papers.
Goodbye to the papers

and to the school for the rich
where I drove them, dressed up
in a tie to declare who I was.

Goodbye to all the ties
and to the life I lost
by declaring, and a fond goodbye

to the two junk cars that lurched
and banged through the campus
making it sure I would never fit in.

Goodbye to the finest campus
money could buy, and one
final goodbye to the paycheck

that was always gone
before I got it home.
Farewell to the home

and a heartfelt goodbye
to all the tenants who rented
the upstairs apartment,

particularly Mrs. Doucette,
whose washer overflowed
down the walls of our bathroom

every other week, and Mr. Green,
determined in spite of the evidence
to learn the electric guitar.

And to you there, the young man
on the roof turning the antenna
and trying not to look down

on how far love has taken you,
and to the faithful wife
in the downstairs window

shouting, "That's as good
as we're going to get it,"
and to the four hopeful children

staying with the whole program
despite the rolling picture
and the snow—goodbye,

wealth and joy to us all
in the new life, goodbye!

# John Hollander

"What's the French for fiddle-de-dee?" "Fiddle-de-dee's
not English," Alice replied gravely. "Whoever said it was,"
said the Red queen . . .


What's the French for "fiddle-de-dee"?
But "fiddle-de-dee's not English" (we
Learn from Alice, and must agree).
The "Fiddle" we know, but what's from "Dee"?
*Le chat assis in an English tree?*


—Well, what's the French for "fiddle-de-dench"?
(That is to say, for "monkey wrench")
—*Once in the works, it produced a stench*


What's the Greek for "fiddle-de-dex"?
(That is to say, for "Brekekekex")
—*The frog-prince turned out to be great at sex.*


What's the Erse for "fiddle-de-derse"?
(That is to say, for "violent curse"?)
—*Bad cess to you for your English verse!*


What's the Malay for "fiddle-de-day"?
(That is to say, for "That is to say . . .")
—*. . .[There are no true synonyms, anyway . . .]*

What's the Pali for "fiddle-de-dally"?
(That is to say, for "Silicon Valley")
—*Maya deceives you: the Nasdaq won't rally.*

What's the Norwegian for "fiddle-de-degian"?
(That is to say, for "His name is Legion")
—*This aquavit's known in every region.*

What's the Punjabi for "fiddle-de-dabi"?
(That is to say, for "crucifer lobby")
—*They asked for dall but were sent kohl-rabi.*

What's the Dutch for "fiddle-de-Dutch"?
(That is to say, for "overmuch")
—*Pea-soup and burghers and tulips and such.*

What's the Farsi for "fiddle-de-darsi?"
(That is to say for "devote yourself"—"darsi"
*In Italian—the Irish would spell it "D'Arcy")*

Well, what's the Italian for "fiddle-de-dallion"?
(That is to say, for "spotted stallion")
—*It makes him more randy to munch on a scallion.*

Having made so free with "fiddle-de-dee,"
What's to become now of "fiddle-de-dum"?
—*I think I know. But the word's still mum.*

## Charles Simic

If you didn't see the six-legged dog,
It doesn't matter.
We did, and he mostly lay in the corner.
As for the extra legs,

One got used to them quickly
And thought of other things.
Like, what a cold, dark night
To be out at the fair.

Then the keeper threw a stick
And the dog went after it
On four legs, the other two flapping behind,
Which made one girl shriek with laughter.

She was drunk and so was the man
Who kept kissing her neck.
The dog got the stick and looked back at us.
And that was the whole show.

# Marie Howe

It was like the moment when a bird decides not to eat
    from your hand,
and flies, just before it flies, the moment the rivers seem
    to still
and stop because a storm is coming, but there is no
    storm, as when
a hundred starlings lift and bank together before they
    wheel and drop,
very much like the moment, driving on bad ice, when it
    occurs to you
your car could spin, just before it slowly begins to spin,
    like
the moment just before you forgot what it was you were
    about to say,
it was like that, and after that, it was still like that, only
all the time.

# Elise Paschen

**BIRTH DAY | 128**

*For Alexandra, born May 17, 1999*

Armored in red, her voice commands
every corner. Bells gong on squares,
in steeples, answering the prayers.
Bright tulips crown the boulevards.

Pulled from the womb she imitates
that mythic kick from some god's head.
She roars, and we are conquered.
Her legs, set free, combat the air.

Naked warrior: she is our own.
Entire empires are overthrown.

## Alison Luterman

I could be the waitress
in the airport restaurant
full of tired cigarette smoke and unseeing tourists.
I could turn into the never-noticed landscape
hanging identically in all the booths
or the customer behind the Chronicle
who has been giving advice about stock portfolios for forty
    years.
I could be his mortal weariness,
his discarded sports section, his smoldering ashtray.
I could be the 70-year-old woman who has never seen
    Hawaii,
touching her red lipstick and sprayed hair.
I could enter the linen dress
that poofs around her body like a bridesmaid,
or become her gay son
sitting opposite her, stirring another sugar
into his coffee for lack of something true to say.
I could be the reincarnated soul of the composer
of the Muzak that plays relentlessly overhead,
or the factory worker who wove this fake Oriental carpet,
or the hushed shoes of the busboy.

But I don't want to be the life of anything in this
    pitstop.

I want to go to Hawaii, the wet, hot
impossible place in my heart that knows just what it
    desires.
I want money, I want candy.
I want sweet ukelele music and birds who drop from the sky.
I want to be the volcano who lavishes
her boiling rock soup love on everyone,
and I want to be the lover
of volcanos, who loves best what burns her as it flows.

# Philip Levine

## THE POEM OF CHALK | 130

On the way to lower Broadway
this morning I faced a tall man
speaking to a piece of chalk
held in his right hand. The left
was open, and it kept the beat,
for his speech had a rhythm,
was a chant or dance, perhaps
even a poem in French, for he
was from Senegal and spoke French
so slowly and precisely that I
could understand as though
hurled back fifty years to my
high school classroom. A slender man,
elegant in his manner, neatly dressed
in the remnants of two blue suits,
his tie fixed squarely, his white shirt
spotless though unironed. He knew
the whole history of chalk, not only
of this particular piece, but also
the chalk with which I wrote
my name the day they welcomed
me back to school after the death
of my father. He knew feldspar,
he knew calcium, oyster shells, he
knew what creatures had given

their spines to become the dust time
pressed into these perfect cones,
he knew the sadness of classrooms
in December when the light fails
early and the words on the blackboard
abandon their grammar and sense
and then even their shapes so that
each letter points in every direction
at once and means nothing at all.
At first I thought his short beard
was frosted with chalk, as we stood
face to face, no more than a foot
apart, I saw the hairs were white,
for though youthful in his gestures
he was, like me, an aging man, though
far nobler in appearance with his high
carved cheekbones, his broad shoulders,
and clear dark eyes. He had the bearing
of a king of lower Broadway, someone
out of the mind of Shakespeare or
García Lorca, someone for whom loss
had sweetened into charity. We stood
for that one long minute, the two
of us sharing the final poem of chalk
while the great city raged around

us, and then the poem ended, as all
poems do, and his left hand dropped
to his side abruptly and he handed
me the piece of chalk. I bowed,
knowing how large a gift this was
and wrote my thanks on the air
where it might be heard forever
below the sea shell's stiffening cry.

*Mark Irwin*

Sunday mornings I would reach
high into his dark closet while standing
         on a chair and tiptoeing reach
higher, touching, sometimes fumbling
         the soft crowns and imagine
I was in a forest, wind hymning
         through pines, where the musky scent
of rain clinging to damp earth was
         his scent I loved, lingering on
bands, leather, and on the inner silk
         crowns where I would smell his
hair and almost think I was being
         held, or climbing a tree, touching
the yellow fruit, leaves whose scent
         was that of clove in the godsome
air, as now, thinking of his fabulous
         sleep, I stand on this canyon floor
and watch light slowly close
         on water I can't be sure is there.

## Norman Dubie

**OF POLITICS & ART** | 132

*for Allen*

Here, on the farthest point of the peninsula
The winter storm
Off the Atlantic shook the schoolhouse.
Mrs. Whitimore, dying
Of tuberculosis, said it would be after dark
Before the snowplow and bus would reach us.

She read to us from Melville.

How in an almost calamitous moment
Of sea hunting
Some men in an open boat suddenly found themselves
At the still and protected center
Of a great herd of whales
Where all the females floated on their sides
While their young nursed there. The cold frightened
    whalers
Just stared into what they allowed
Was the ecstatic lapidary pond of a nursing cow's
One visible eyeball.
And they were at peace with themselves.

Today I listened to a woman say
That Melville *might*

Be taught in the next decade. Another woman asked, "And
    why not?"
The first responded, "Because there are
No women in his one novel."

And Mrs. Whitimore was now reading from the Psalms.
Coughing into her handkerchief. Snow above the
    windows.
There was a blue light on her face, breasts, and arms.
Sometimes a whole civilization can be dying
Peacefully in one young woman, in a small heated room
With thirty children
Rapt, confident and listening to the pure
God-rendering voice of a storm.

# Stephen Dobyns

## LOUD MUSIC | 133

My stepdaughter and I circle round and round.
You see, I like the music loud, the speakers
throbbing, jam-packing the room with sound whether
Bach or rock and roll, the volume cranked up so
each bass note is like a hand smacking the gut.
But my stepdaughter disagrees. She is four
and likes the music decorous, pitched below
her own voice—that tenuous projection of self.
With music blasting, she feels she disappears,
is lost within the blare, which in fact I like.
But at four what she wants is self-location
and uses her voice as a porpoise uses
its sonar: to find herself in all this space.
If she had a sort of box with a peephole
and looked inside, what she'd like to see would be
herself standing there in her red pants, jacket,
yellow plastic lunch box: a proper subject
for serious study. But me, if I raised
the same box to my eye, I would wish to find
the ocean on one of those days when wind
and thick cloud make the water gray and restless
as if some creature brooded underneath,
a rocky coast with a road along the shore
where someone like me was walking and has gone.

Loud music does this, it wipes out the ego,
leaving turbulent water and winding road,
a landscape stripped of people and language—
how clear the air becomes, how sharp the colors.

# Henry Taylor

## ELEVATOR MUSIC | 134

A tune with no more substance than the air,
performed on underwater instruments,
is proper to this short lift from the earth.
It hovers as we draw into ourselves
and turn our reverent eyes toward the lights
that count us to our various destinies.
We're all in this together, the song says,
and later we'll descend. The melody
is like a name we don't recall just now
that still keeps on insisting it is there.

# Nancy Willard

Who is this fish, still wearing its wealth,
flat on my drainboard, dead asleep,
its suit of mail proof only against the stream?
What is it to live in a stream,
to dwell forever in a tunnel of cold,
never to leave your shining birthsuit,
never to spend your inheritance of thin coins?
And who is the stream, who lolls all day
in an unmade bed, living on nothing but weather,
singing, a little mad in the head,
opening her apron to shells, carcasses, crabs,
eyeglasses, the lines of fisherman begging for
news from the interior—oh, who are these lines
that link a big sky to a small stream
that go down for great things:
the cold muscle of the trout,
the shining scrawl of the eel in a difficult passage,
hooked—but who is this hook, this cunning
and faithful fanatic who will not let go
but holds the false bait and the true worm alike
and tears the fish, yet gives it up to the basket
in which it will ride to the kitchen
of someone important, perhaps the Pope
who rejoices that his cook has found such a fish
and blesses it and eats it and rises, saying,

"Children, what is it to live in the stream,
day after day, and come at last to the table,
transfigured with spices and herbs,
a little martyr, a little miracle;
children, children, who is this fish?"

# Evie Shockley

i cop a squat on a squared-off log,
to watch you ball on the community center court.
butt numb, i shift my weight

and shake mosquitos from my ankles,
but never take my eyes off the game.
yours follow the orange orb, your pupils
twin, brown moons reflecting its light.

your play is wild efficiency,
you are a four-pronged magic wand,
waving, as if agentless, in all directions at once.
an opponent dribbles the ball—now he sees it,

now he don't, it's gone, flown,
and you've given it its wings.
you are one-eighth of the shrieking rubber,

one-eighth of the growls and calls. you are
the delicious assist, the unerring pass.
you spread your skills out before me, a peacock
among pigeons, as if to say "all eyes on me,"

and make it worth my while.
a chill trails the sun west like a long, clammy train,

crawls over me and my makeshift bench,
over the emptying playground,

but stops at the edge of the concrete,
where eight men burning keep it at bay,
the way torches smoking around a patio

ward off insects. twilight rises like dark steam
from the dewy grass, but you don't see it.
the ball still lights the court
until the winning jumper sinks and puts it out.

then earth returns to view, and you jog over
to slap my palm and beam,
and receive the grin i give you like a trophy.

My half-brother had dark sad eyes, wheaten hair
and the same gorgeous skin his mother had.
He was cute and smart and innately kind,
unlike me at his age, according to our father.
Five years younger than me,
Tim attracted all the love
my father had frozen in his heart
when I was growing up.
Tim was brought up on my old books.
He did better than I with poetry,
reciting by six some "grownup" verses
which I couldn't memorize at eleven.
At eight he wrote a poem
at the back of his math exercise book
and forgot about it.
It was a love poem
with an underlined dedication, "To A."
It so happened that I knew who A was.
The poem read as follows:
"I loved and missed her so much
that I forgot what she looked like,
and when she entered the classroom
in the morning, I did not recognize her.
I did not recognize her long face,
nor her slow neck, nor her skinny hands,

I had completely forgotten her green eyes."
It was quite a work of art, in my opinion,
but I told him that to sigh about
legs and necks and eyes
was sentimental and girlish.
He listened to me with dry eyes
and then tore out the page and threw it away
into the wastebasket.
He never wrote poetry again, but I did.
At fifteen I wrote a short story
which had some success and was even
published in a teenage literary magazine
called "Asterisks." It was around that time
that I stopped visiting my dad's house
after I realized
that everything about this boy
put me down, humiliated me
and filled me with jealousy.
I would meet with dad on one condition:
if he wanted to see me,
he had to come to my place
or to stop by at the artsy cafe,
where my older friend Lena and I
would go after school
to sip strawberry milkshakes.

One day my father
came to my school during class hours
to take me to a hospital: the night before
my half-brother had gotten sick.
We arrived in the middle of the doctor's rounds.
The waiting area was noisy
and smelled of urine and medication.
Dad had gone inside,
I waited for him to call me in.
Through the door left ajar
I saw a row of iron bunks with striped mattresses.
Tim's was next to the door.
He lay leaning on a big gray pillow,
a glass of water in his hand.
The doctor wanted him to take a pill,
but he wouldn't hear of it.
He was willful, obstreperous,
he pushed away the hand of medicine.
"I want that ship, that ship . . ." he whined.
"What ship?" My father turned pale
and stared at the doctor. "Can't you see?
The green one, over there!" cried Tim,
inserting his finger in the glass of water
where a green ship, a three-funneled steamer,
was slowly sinking at the time.

# Bruce Weigl

I wanted to stay with my dog
when they did her in
I told the young veterinarian
who wasn't surprised.
Shivering on the chrome table,
she did not raise her eyes to me when I came in.
Something was resolved in her.
Some darkness exchanged for the pain.
There were a few more words
about the size of her tumor and her age,
and how we wanted to stop her suffering,
or our own, or stop all suffering
from happening before us
and then the nurse shaved May's skinny leg
with those black clippers;
she passed the needle to the doctor
and for once I knew what to do
and held her head against mine.
I cleaved to that smell
and lied into her ear
that it would be all right.
The veterinarian, whom I'd fought
about when to do this thing
said through tears
that it would take only a few minutes

as if that were not a long time
but there was no cry or growl,
only the weight of her in my arms,
and then on the world.

# Sharon Olds

The day my girl is lost for an hour,
the day I think she is gone forever and then I find her,
I sit with her awhile and then I
go to the corner store for orange juice for her
lips, tongue, palate, throat,
stomach, blood, every gold cell of her body.
I joke around with the guy behind the counter, I
walk out into the winter air and
weep. I know he would never hurt her,
never take her body in his hands to
crack it or crush it, would keep her safe and
bring her home to me. Yet there are
those who would. I pass the huge
cockeyed buildings massive as prisons,
charged, loaded, cocked with people,
some who would love to take my girl, to un-
do her, fine strand by fine
strand. These are buildings full of rope,
ironing boards, sash, wire,
iron cords woven in black-and-blue spirals like
umbilici, apartments supplied with
razor blades and lye. This is my
quest, to know where it is, the evil in the
human heart. As I walk home I
look in face after face for it, I

see the dark beauty, the rage, the
grown-up children of the city she walks as a
child, a raw target. I cannot
see a soul who would do it, I clutch the
jar of juice like a cold heart,
remembering the time my parents tied me to a chair and
would not feed me and I looked up
into their beautiful faces, my stomach a
bright mace, my wrists like birds the
shrike has hung by the throat from barbed wire, I
gazed as deep as I could into their eyes
and all I saw was goodness, I could not get past it.
I rush home with the blood of oranges
pressed to my breast, I cannot get it to her fast enough.

# Timothy Russell

When she stopped on the sidewalk,
near the yellow storm drain,
near gnats swarming above the hedge,
the little girl, perhaps three,
yelled something unintelligible
at the doll in the pink carriage.
When she slapped her baby
I remembered flocks of pigeons
erupting from beams and ledges
at the Sinter Plant,
how they would flutter and circle,
flickering in the sun, and always
return to their niches to roost.

Another word for *father* is *worry*.

Worry boils the water
for tea in the middle of the night.

Worry trimmed the child's nails before
singing him to sleep.

Another word for *son* is *delight*,
another word, *hidden*.

And another is *One-Who-Goes-Away*.
Yet another, *One-Who-Returns*.

So many words for son:
*He-Dreams-for-All-Our-Sakes*.
*His-Play-Vouchsafes-Our-Winter-Share*.
*His-Dispersal-Wins-the-Birds*.

But only one word for *father*.
And sometimes a man is both.
Which is to say sometimes a man
manifests mysteries beyond
his own understanding.

# David Hilton

Others always skip over the word
That will bring the belligerents of the world
To the negotiating table, if only

I can get it written, or will
Teach thin kids in Woetown, West Virginia,
To rebound tough and read Ted Roethke—

I'm writing along in a conspiracy
Of birds and sun and pom-pom girls
Lines to cheer old ladies with shopping bags

Waiting by their busstops at 5PM
Or lines to get the 12-year-olds off cigarettes
Or save the suicides in gay-bar mensrooms

Or save the fat man from his refrigerator
Or the brilliant boy from color TV
Or the RA private from re-upping for six

Or the whole Midwest from wanting to conquer Asia and
    the Moon
Or the current president from his place in history—
Oh, if only I can get it written

No one will burn kittens or slap little boys or make little
    girls cry
Or cower at cancer or coronaries or plain palsied old age
Or get goofy from radiation in his cornflake milk—

If only I can get it written. But always
When I get close to the word and the crowd begins to roar
The common pen skips, leaves the page blank—

But you, BIC pen, at nineteen cents, could trace truce
    terms on tank treads,
Could ratify in the most flourishing script
The amnesty of love for our most dreaded enemies:

The ugly, the poor, the stupid, the sexually screwed-up—
Etching their releases across the slippery communiqués
    of generals and governors,
For Behold you can write upon butter, Yea inscribe
    even through slime!

But at nineteen cents no one pays attention
To the deadwood you shatter or the manifestoes you slice
    in the ice—
For who would believe Truth at *that* price.

*Robert Wrigley*

So here is the old buck
    who all winter long
had traveled with the does
    and yearlings, with the fawns
just past their spots,
    and who had hung back,
walking where the others had walked,
    eating what they had left,
and who had struck now and then
    a pose against the wind,
against a twig-snap or the way
    the light came slinking
among the trees.

Here is the mangled ear
    and the twisted, hindering leg.
Here, already bearing him away
    among the last drifts of snow
and the nightly hard freezes,
    is a line of tiny ants,
making its way from the cave
    of the right eye, over the steep
occipital ridge, across the moonscape, shed-horn
    medallion and through the valley

of the ear's cloven shadow
      to the ground,
where among the staves
      of shed needles and the red earthy wine
they carry him
      bit by gnawn bit
into another world.

# Steve Kowit

A noun's a thing. A verb's the thing it does.
An adjective is what describes the noun.
In "The can of beets is filled with purple fuzz"

*of* and *with* are prepositions. *The*'s
an article, a *can*'s a noun,
a noun's a thing. A verb's the thing it does.

A can *can* roll—or not. What isn't was
or might be, *might* meaning not yet known.
"Our can of beets *is* filled with purple fuzz"

is present tense. While words like our and us
are pronouns—i.e. *it* is moldy, *they* are icky brown.
A noun's a thing; a verb's the thing it does.

*Is* is a helping verb. It helps because
*filled* isn't a full verb. *Can*'s what *our* owns
in "Our can of beets is filled with purple fuzz."

See? There's almost nothing to it. Just
memorize these rules . . . or write them down!
A noun's a thing, a verb's the thing it does.
The can of beets is filled with purple fuzz.

# Edward Hirsch

**FAST BREAK** | 145

*In Memory of Dennis Turner, 1946–1984*

A hook shot kisses the rim and
hangs there, helplessly, but doesn't drop,

and for once our gangly starting center
boxes out his man and times his jump

perfectly, gathering the orange leather
from the air like a cherished possession

and spinning around to throw a strike
to the outlet who is already shoveling

an underhand pass toward the other guard
scissoring past a flat-footed defender

who looks stunned and nailed to the floor
in the wrong direction, trying to catch sight

of a high, gliding dribble and a man
letting the play develop in front of him

in slow motion, almost exactly
like a coach's drawing on the blackboard,

both forwards racing down the court
the way that forwards should, fanning out

and filling the lanes in tandem, moving
together as brothers passing the ball

between them without a dribble, without
a single bounce hitting the hardwood

until the guard finally lunges out
and commits to the wrong man

while the power-forward explodes past them
in a fury, taking the ball into the air

by himself now and laying it gently
against the glass for a lay-up,

but losing his balance in the process,
inexplicably falling, hitting the floor

with a wild, headlong motion
for the game he loved like a country

and swiveling back to see an orange blur
floating perfectly though the net.

# Dean Young

The mind becomes a field of snow
but then the snow melts and dandelions
blink on and you can walk through them,
your trousers plastered with dew.
They're all waiting for you but first
here's a booth where you can win

a peacock feather for bursting a balloon,
a man in huge stripes shouting about
a boy who is half swan, the biggest
pig in the world. Then you will pass
tractors pulling other tractors,
trees snagged with bright wrappers

and then you will come to a river
and then you will wash your face.

# Gary Soto

I was hoping to be happy by seventeen.
School was a sharp check mark in the roll book,
An obnoxious tuba playing at noon because our team
Was going to win at night. The teachers were
Too close to dying to understand. The hallways
Stank of poor grades and unwashed hair. Thus,
A friend and I sat watching the water on Saturday,
Neither of us talking much, just warming ourselves
By hurling large rocks at the dusty ground
And feeling awful because San Francisco was a postcard
On a bedroom wall. We wanted to go there,
Hitchhike under the last migrating birds
And be with people who knew more than three chords
On a guitar. We didn't drink or smoke,
But our hair was shoulder length, wild when
The wind picked up and the shadows of
This loneliness gripped loose dirt. By bus or car,
By the sway of train over a long bridge,
We wanted to get out. The years froze
As we sat on the bank. Our eyes followed the water,
White-tipped but dark underneath, racing out of town.

# David Ray

Doing without
    is an interesting
custom, involving such in-
    visible items as the food
that's not on the table, the clothes
    that are not on the back
the radio whose only music
    is silence. Doing without
is a great protector of reputations
    since all places one cannot go
are fabulous, and only the rare and
    enlightened plowman in his field
or on his mountain does not overrate
    what he does not or cannot have.
Saluting through their windows
    of cathedral glass those restaurants
we must not enter (unless like
    burglars we become subject to
arrest) we greet with our twinkling
    eyes the faces of others who do
without, the lady with the
    fishing pole, and the man who looks
amused to have discovered on a walk
    another piece of firewood.

# Charles Webb

## THE DEATH OF SANTA CLAUS | 149

He's had the chest pains for weeks,
but doctors don't make house
calls to the North Pole,

he's let his Blue Cross lapse,
blood tests make him faint,
hospital gowns always flap

open, waiting rooms upset
his stomach, and it's only
indigestion anyway, he thinks,

until, feeding the reindeer,
he feels as if a monster fist
has grabbed his heart and won't

stop squeezing. He can't
breathe, and the beautiful white
world he loves goes black,

and he drops on his jelly belly
in the snow and Mrs. Claus
tears out of the toy factory

wailing, and the elves wring
their little hands, and Rudolph's
nose blinks like a sad ambulance

light, and in a tract house
in Houston, Texas, I'm 8,
telling my mom that stupid

kids at school say Santa's a big
fake, and she sits with me
on our purple-flowered couch,

and takes my hand, tears
in her throat, the terrible
news rising in her eyes.

## Ron Padgett

### LADIES AND GENTLEMEN
### IN OUTER SPACE | 150

Here is my philosophy:
Everything changes (the word "everything"
has just changed as the
word "change" has: it now
means "no change") so
quickly that it literally surpasses my belief,
charges right past it
like some of the giant
ideas in this area.
I had no beginning and I shall have
no end: the beam of light
stretches out before and behind
and I cook the vegetables
for a few minutes only,
the fewer the better. Butter
and serve. Here is my
philosophy: butter and serve.

# Mac Hammond

The man who stands above the bird, his knife
Sharp as a Turkish scimitar, first removes
A thigh and leg, half the support
On which the turkey used to stand. This
Leg and thigh he sets on an extra
Plate. All his weight now on
One leg, he lunges for the wing, the wing
On the same side of the bird from which
He has just removed the leg and thigh.
He frees the wing enough to expose
The breast, the wing not severed but
Collapsed down to the platter. One hand
Holding the fork, piercing the turkey
Anywhere, he now begins to slice the breast,
Afflicted by small pains in his chest,
A kind of heartburn for which there is no
Cure. He serves the hostess breast, her
Own breast rising and falling. And so on,
Till all the guests are served, the turkey
Now a wreck, the carver exhausted, a
Mere carcass of his former self. Everyone
Says thanks to the turkey carver and begins
To eat, thankful for the cold turkey
And the Republic for which it stands.

# John Updike

She must have been kicked unseen or brushed by a car.
Too young to know much, she was beginning to learn
To use the newspapers spread on the kitchen floor
And to win, wetting there, the words, "Good dog! Good
    dog!"

We thought her shy malaise was a shot reaction.
The autopsy disclosed a rupture in her liver.
As we teased her with play, blood was filling her skin
And her heart was learning to lie down forever.

Monday morning, as the children were noisily fed
And sent to school, she crawled beneath the youngest's bed.
We found her twisted limp but still alive.
In the car to the vet's, on my lap, she tried

To bite my hand and died. I stroked her warm fur
And my wife called in a voice imperious with tears.
Though surrounded by love that would have upheld her,
Nevertheless she sank and, stiffening, disappeared.

Back home, we found that in the night her frame,
Drawing near to dissolution, had endured the shame
Of diarrhoea and had dragged across the floor
To a newspaper carelessly left there. *Good dog.*

# Donald Finkel

Three nights in a row
he fed on our leavings
rattling our cans
till we let him in

wherever we went, he went
to the end of his rope

we let him in
we let him out
we let him in again

one night at the corner, he paused
the old bones squared
his ears cocked soft to hear
what it said, it said
nothing I could hear

in the streetlight his life
hung loose on his bones
a hammock of shadow

we let him out
we let him in
we let him out again

## Martha McFerren

Sometimes super cool
is nothing more than
pure preparedness.
Like my friend Janet
who was terrified
someday she'd swerve
to miss a dog
and demolish her car
and kill herself
and maybe her children.
For years, whenever
she got behind a wheel
she was thinking,
*Hit the dog, hit the dog,*
and finally one night
the dog got there
and she slammed
flat across him.

I cried real tears
when Lassie came home,
but I'm worth something, too.
Let's both watch out, dog.

# Ruth L. Schwartz

Isn't one of your prissy richpeoples' swans
Wouldn't be at home on some pristine pond
Chooses the whole stinking shoreline, candy wrappers,
condoms
      in its tidal fringe
Prefers to curve its muscular, slightly grubby neck
      into the body of a Great Lake,
Swilling whatever it is swans swill,
Chardonnay of algae with bouquet of crud,
While Clevelanders walk by saying Look
      at that big duck!
Beauty isn't the point here; of course
      the swan is beautiful,
But not like Lorie at 16, when
Everything was possible—no
More like Lorie at 27
Smoking away her days off in her dirty kitchen,
Her kid with asthma watching TV,
The boyfriend who doesn't know yet she's gonna
Leave him, washing his car out back—and
He's a runty little guy, and drinks too much, and
It's not his kid anyway, but he loves her, he
Really does, he loves them both—
That's the kind of swan this is.

## Phillis Levin

### THE BLIZZARD | 156

Now that the worst is over, they predict
Something messy and difficult, though not
Life-threatening. Clearly we needed

To stock up on water and candles, making
Tureens of soup and things that keep
When electricity fails and phone lines fall.

Igloos rise on air conditioners, gargoyles
Fly and icicles shatter. Frozen runways,
Lines in markets, and paralyzed avenues

Verify every fear. But there is warmth
In this sudden desire to sleep,
To surrender to our common condition

With joy, watching hours of news
Devoted to weather. People finally stop
To talk to each other—the neighbors

We didn't know were always here.
Today they are ready for business,
Armed with a new vocabulary,

Casting their saga in phrases as severe
As last night's snow: *damage assessment,*
*Evacuation, emergency management.*

The shift of the wind matters again,
And we are so simple, so happy to hear
The scrape of a shovel next door.

# Peter Cherches

Where is she, I wondered, when she wasn't there. If she's not here she could be anywhere. She could be anywhere and not alone.

I began to imagine the worst. At every imagining I thought I had imagined the worst, then I imagined something even worse. It got to the point where my imaginings no longer included her. I realized that the worst did not encompass her. As my imaginings continued, as worst superseded worst, making the preceding worst only worse, I began to forget her. As worst got worse, I forgot her more. Things were getting pretty bad, and I had almost forgotten her completely, when she reappeared.

## Alberto Ríos

It was afternoon tea, with tea foods spread out
Like in the books, except that it was coffee.

She made a tin pot of cowboy coffee, from memory,
*That's what we used to call it*, she said, *cowboy coffee.*

The grounds she pinched up in her hands, not a spoon,
And the fire on the stove she made from a match.

I sat with her and talked, but the talk was like the tea food,
A little of this and something from the other plate as well,

Always with a napkin and a thank-you. We sat and visited
And I watched her smoke cigarettes

Until the afternoon light was funny in the room,
And then we said our good-byes. The visit was liniment,

The way the tea was coffee, a confusion plain and nice,
A balm for the nerves of two people living in the world,

A balm in the tenor of its language, which spoke through
    our hands
In the small lifting of our cups and our cakes to our lips.

It was simplicity, and held only what it needed.
It was a gentle visit, and I did not see her again.

# Eamon Grennan

Looking for distinctive stones, I found the dead otter
rotting by the tideline, and carried all day the scent of
    this savage
valediction. That headlong high sound the oystercatcher
    makes
came echoing through the rocky cove
where a cormorant was feeding and submarining in the bay
and a heron rose off a boulder where he'd been invisible,
drifted a little, stood again—a hieroglyph
or just longevity reflecting on itself
between the sky clouding over and the lightly ruffled
    water.

This was the morning after your dream of dying, of being
    held
and told it didn't matter. A butterfly went jinking over
the wave-silky stones, and where I turned
to go up the road again, a couple in a blue camper sat
smoking their cigarettes over their breakfast coffee (blue
scent of smoke, the thick dark smell of fresh coffee)
and talking in quiet voices, first one then the other
    answering,
their radio telling the daily news behind them. It was
    warm.
All seemed at peace. I could feel the sun coming off the
    water.

# Miller Williams

I think the death of domestic animals
marks the sea changes in our lives.
Think how things were, when things were different.
There was an animal then, a dog or a cat,
not the one you have now, another one.
Think when things were different before that.
There was another one then. You had almost forgotten.

# Kaylin Haught

I asked God if it was okay to be melodramatic
and she said yes
I asked her if it was okay to be short
and she said it sure is
I asked her if I could wear nail polish
or not wear nail polish
and she said honey
she calls me that sometimes
she said you can do just exactly
what you want to
Thanks God I said
And is it even okay if I don't paragraph
my letters
Sweetcakes God said
who knows where she picked that up
what I'm telling you is
Yes Yes Yes

*Shara McCallum*

I am alone in the garden, separated
from my class. This is what comes
of trying to make the perfect heart.

Scissors: silvery cold and slipping
through my four-year-old fingers.
I did not know and took the harder route,

tried to carve a mirrored mountain top
from each center of the page
after page of red construction paper.

Now, I am counting the frangipani
in bloom. Teacher's words still shriller
than the mockingbird's. My cheeks,

wet and hot from more than heat.
If I had been taught, if
once I had been shown the way,

I would have obeyed—not been
a *spoiled, rude, wasteful little girl.*
Folding the paper in two,
I would have cut away the crescent moon.

# Elizabeth Seydel Morgan

## THE BIRTHDAY | 163

I'm driving tonight into November.
The cold black sky is coming at me
and before I know it
it snuffs out the gold October glow
I left behind in Charlottesville,
those calendar leaves, the big ball sun
setting behind the rolling steeplechase—
its little obstacles casting shadows—
the lighted windows on the darkening hill,
silhouettes of hosts in my rearview mirror,
the last orange light on Foxfield Road.
Into the dark I can speed east and think
of the last night in October, Halloween,
when you were born thirty years ago.

Or I could not think of that night,
I know you'll be glad if I don't. It's still
today in Los Angeles, you're looking
for work. We're both looking for work
to keep us in days to get up.
I like this night highway blacking out
autumn, making us one with all seasons.
Only my headlights and pairs of red taillights
ahead, you turning thirty where the leaves never
fall, the children not masked yet, the last sun
of the month still in the sky.

I drive toward distant clouds and my mother's dying.
The quickened sky is mercury, it slithers
across the horizon. Against that liquid silence,
a V of birds crosses—sudden and silver.

They tilt, becoming white light as they turn, glitter
like shooting stars arcing slow motion out of the abyss,
not falling.
                    Now they look like chips of flint,
the arrow broken.
                    I think, This isn't myth—
they are not signs, not souls.
                                        Reaching blue
again, they're ordinary ducks or maybe
Canada geese. Veering away they shoot
into the west, too far for my eyes, aching

as they do.

          Never mind what I said
before. Those birds took my breath. I knew what it meant.

## Robley Wilson

### I WISH IN THE CITY OF
### YOUR HEART | 165

I wish in the city of your heart
you would let me be the street
where you walk when you are most
yourself. I imagine the houses:
It has been raining, but the rain
is done and the children kept home
have begun opening their doors.

Don't play too much, don't play
too loud, don't play the melody.
You have to anticipate her
and to subdue yourself.
She used to give me her smoky
eye when I got boisterous,
so I learned to play on tip-
toe and to play the better half
of what I might. I don't like
to complain, though I notice
that I get around to it somehow.
We made a living and good music,
both, night after night, the blue
curlicues of smoke rubbing their
staling and wispy backs
against the ceilings, the flat
drinks and scarce taxis, the jazz life
we bitch about the way Army pals
complain about the food and then
re-up. Some people like to say
with smut in their voices how playing
the way we did at our best is partly
sexual. OK, I could tell them
a tale or two, and I've heard
the records Lester cut with Lady Day

and all that rap, and it's partly
sexual but it's mostly practice
and music. As for partly sexual,
I'll take wholly sexual any day,
but that's a duet and we're talking
accompaniment. Remember "Reckless
Blues"? Bessie Smith sings out "Daddy"
and Louis Armstrong plays back "Daddy"
as clear through his horn as if he'd
spoken it. But it's her daddy and her
story. When you play it you become
your part in it, one of her beautiful
troubles, and then, however much music
can do this, part of her consolation,
the way pain and joy eat off each other's
plates, but mostly you play to drunks,
to the night, to the way you judge
and pardon yourself, to all that goes
not unsung, but unrecorded.

Not the walls of the furled city,
through which he drifted like malign sleet,
nor every vigilance, could stop him.
He came and rent some poor soul
to morsels and ate him. There was no help
nearby, so St. Francis slogged
from Assisi to tame the wolf.
Sassetta painted this meeting.
The wolf, pert and teachable as Lassie,
has laid his licentious, vow-making right paw
in the saint's hand and meets with his
ochre eye the saint's chastening gaze.
The townspeople stand like a grove
and watch. Probably one of their faces
belonged to a patron who commissioned
Sassetta, but which face? Art remembers
a few things by forgetting many.
The wolf lived on in the nearby hills
but never ate, the story goes, another
citizen. Was Sassetta the last one,
then, to see on the piazza, like dropped
firewood, most of a leg and what may be
a forearm gnawed from both ends, lurid
with scarlet blood? None in the painting
looks at this carnage and bright waste,

nor thinks of the gnarled woods
in which the pewter-colored wolf
makes his huge home, nor measures with what work
each stone was prized from the furious ground
to build each house in Gubbio
and to lay a piazza atop the town
and to raise above it a tower.

## Samuel Menashe

I close my eyes
Avoid the rush
Sometimes I doze
Inside the bus
If I arrive
At six-fifteen
Will I be seen?
Seven times seven
Makes forty-nine
Even at eleven
I was on time

# Marie Howe

No matter how many times I try I can't stop my father
from walking into my sister's room

and I can't see any better, leaning from here to look
in his eyes. It's dark in the hall

and everyone's sleeping. This is the past
where everything is perfect already and nothing changes,

where the water glass falls to the bathroom floor
and bounces once before breaking.

Nothing. Not the small sound my sister makes, turning
over, not the thump of the dog's tail

when he opens one eye to see him stumbling back to bed
still drunk, a little bewildered.

This is exactly as I knew it would be.
And if I whisper her name, hissing a warning,

I've been doing that for years now, and still the dog
startles and growls until he sees

it's our father, and still the door opens, and she
makes that small *oh* turning over.

Once the world was waiting for a song
when along came this. Some said it was a joke
funny ha-ha but at the end too lachrymose
to last. Others that it was writ
holier than thou and should be catechized,
then set to turgid dirges, wept over
with gnashed fang, wrung palm.
The ancient declaimed it fad,
the young, old fogies' play.
Almost everyone agreed, except the children,
who didn't listen, it was kid stuff.


Centuries yawned and fell back, stuporous,
eons stretched out, soaking up beauty sleep.
Then one day a peasant, knowing he hurt too much,
remembered hurting too much, told his wife
he might have written it
if, in another life, he'd been born better,
at least literate.
And when the gods heard this
they hungered suddenly to become mortal
and join themselves with us in lecherous praise.
Thus hereafter follows the stories of their sins,
their cries made flesh by euphony and trope
they whispered to us that we take them down,

their great debauches, all made up
that we should emulate with our blood, pay in blood,
while they in the cheap seats, stomp the floor and clap—
all loss, all the fallible, all poetry.

# Susan Mitchell

At night the dead come down to the river to drink.
They unburden themselves of their fears,
their worries for us. They take out the old photographs.
They pat the lines in our hands and tell our futures,
which are cracked and yellow.
Some dead find their way to our houses.
They go up to the attics.
They read the letters they sent us, insatiable
for signs of their love.
They tell each other stories.
They make so much noise
they wake us
as they did when we were children and they stayed up
drinking all night in the kitchen.

# Terence Winch

No one is safe. The streets are unsafe.
Even in the safety zones, it's not safe.
Even safe sex is not safe.
Even things you lock up in a safe
are not safe. Never deposit anything
in a safe-deposit box, because it
won't be safe there. Nobody is safe
at home during baseball games anymore.

At night I go around in the dark
locking everything, returning
a few minutes later
to make sure I locked
everything. It's not safe here.
It's not safe and they know it.
People get hurt using safety pins.

It was not always this way.
Long ago, everyone felt safe. Aristotle
never felt danger. Herodotus felt danger
only when Xerxes was around. Young women
were afraid of wingèd dragons, but felt
relaxed otherwise. Timotheus, however,
was terrified of storms until he played
one on the flute. After that, everyone

was more afraid of him than of the violent
west wind, which was fine with Timotheus.
Euclid, full of music himself, believed only
that there was safety in numbers.

# Ronald Wallace

## THE STUDENT THEME | 173

The adjectives all ganged up on the nouns,
insistent, loud, demanding, inexact,
their Latinate constructions flashing. The pronouns
lost their referents: They were dangling, lacked
the stamina to follow the prepositions' lead
in, on, into, to, toward, for, or from.
They were beset by passive voices and dead
metaphors, conjunctions shouting *But!* or *And!*

The active verbs were all routinely modified
by adverbs, that endlessly and colorlessly ran
into trouble with the participles sitting
on the margins knitting their brows like gerunds
(dangling was their problem, too). The author
was nowhere to be seen; was off somewhere.

## Douglas Goetsch

### SMELL AND ENVY | 174

You nature poets think you've got it, hostaged
somewhere in Vermont or Oregon,
so it blooms and withers only for you,
so all you have to do is name it: primrose
—and now you're writing poetry, and now
you ship it off to us, to smell and envy.

But we are made of newspaper and smoke
and we dunk your roses in vats of blue.
Birds don't call, our pigeons play it close
to the vest. When the moon is full
we hear it in the sirens. The Pleiades
you could probably buy downtown. Gravity
is the receiver on the hook. Mortality
we smell on certain people as they pass.

# Paul Blackburn

**THE YAWN** | 175

The black-haired girl
with the big

                brown

                          eyes
on the Queen's train coming

                  in to work, so
opens her mouth so beautifully

                wide

                        in a ya-aawn, that
two stops after she has left the train
I have only to think of her       and I

      o-oh-aaaww-hm

      wow       !

# Jody Gladding

BLUE WILLOW | 176

A pond will deepen toward the center like a plate
we traced its shallow rim my mother steering
my inner tube past the rushes where I looked
for Moses we said it was a trip around the world
in China we wove through curtains of willow
that tickled our necks let's do that again
and we'd double back idle there lifting
our heads to the green rain
swallows met over us later I dreamed
of flying with them we had all the time
in the world we had the world
how could those trees be weeping?

# Denver Butson

A man standing at the bus stop
reading the newspaper is on fire
Flames are peeking out
from beneath his collar and cuffs
His shoes have begun to melt

The woman next to him
wants to mention it to him
that he is burning
but she is drowning
Water is everywhere
in her mouth and ears
in her eyes
A stream of water runs
steadily from her blouse

Another woman stands at the bus stop
freezing to death
She tries to stand near the man
who is on fire
to try to melt the icicles
that have formed on her eyelashes
and on her nostrils
to stop her teeth long enough
from chattering to say something

to the woman who is drowning
but the woman who is freezing to death
has trouble moving
with blocks of ice on her feet

It takes the three some time
to board the bus
what with the flames
and water and ice
But when they finally climb the stairs
and take their seats
the driver doesn't even notice
that none of them has paid
because he is tortured
by visions and is wondering
if the man who got off at the last stop
was really being mauled to death
by wild dogs.

# Naomi Lazard

Welcome to you
who have managed to get here.
It's been a terrible trip;
you should be happy you have survived it.
Statistics prove that not many do.
You would like a bath, a hot meal,
a good night's sleep. Some of you
need medical attention.
None of this is available.
These things have always been
in short supply; now
they are impossible to obtain.

                               This is not
a temporary situation;
it is permanent.
Our condolences on your disappointment.
It is not our responsibility
everything you have heard about this place
is false. It is not our fault
you have been deceived,
ruined your health getting here.
For reasons beyond our control
there is no vehicle out.

# Gerald Stern

I am going to carry my bed into New York City tonight
complete with dangling sheets and ripped blankets;
I am going to push it across three dark highways
or coast along under 600,000 faint stars.
I want to have it with me so I don't have to beg
for too much shelter from my weak and exhausted friends.
I want to be as close as possible to my pillow
in case a dream or a fantasy should pass by.
I want to fall asleep on my own fire escape
and wake up dazed and hungry
to the sound of garbage grinding in the street below
and the smell of coffee cooking in the window above.

# Heather McHugh

## WHAT HE THOUGHT | 180

*for Fabbio Doplicher*

We were supposed to do a job in Italy
and, full of our feeling for
ourselves (our sense of being
Poets from America) we went
from Rome to Fano, met
the mayor, mulled
a couple matters over (what's
cheap date, they asked us; what's
flat drink). Among Italian literati

we could recognize our counterparts:
the academic, the apologist,
the arrogant, the amorous,
the brazen and the glib—and there was one

administrator (the conservative), in suit
of regulation gray, who like a good tour guide
with measured pace and uninflected tone narrated
sights and histories the hired van hauled us past.
Of all, he was most politic and least poetic,
so it seemed. Our last few days in Rome
(when all but three of the New World Bards had flown)
I found a book of poems this

unprepossessing one had written: it was there
in the *pensione* room (a room he'd recommended)
where it must have been abandoned by
the German visitor (was there a bus of *them*?)
to whom he had inscribed and dated it a month before.
I couldn't read Italian, either, so I put the book
back into the wardrobe's dark. We last Americans

were due to leave tomorrow. For our parting evening then
our host chose something in a family restaurant, and
    there
we sat and chatted, sat and chewed,
till, sensible it was our last
big chance to be poetic, make
our mark, one of us asked
                "What's poetry?
Is it the fruits and vegetables and
marketplace of Campo dei Fiori, or
the statue there?" Because I was

the glib one, I identified the answer
instantly, I didn't have to think—"The truth
is both, it's both," I blurted out. But that
was easy. That was easiest to say. What followed

taught me something about difficulty,
for our underestimated host spoke out,
all of a sudden, with a rising passion, and he said:

The statue represents Giordano Bruno,
brought to be burned in the public square
because of his offense against
authority, which is to say
the Church. His crime was his belief
the universe does not revolve around
the human being: God is no
fixed point or central government, but rather is
poured in waves through all things. All things
move. "If God is not the soul itself, He is
the soul of the soul of the world." Such was
his heresy. The day they brought him
forth to die, they feared he might
incite the crowd (the man was famous
for his eloquence). And so his captors
placed upon his face
an iron mask, in which

he could not speak. That's
how they burned him. That is how

he died: without a word, in front
of everyone.

               And poetry—

                           (we'd all
put down our forks by now, to listen to
the man in gray; he went on
softly)—

          poetry is what
he thought, but did not say.

## notes on the contributors

**Sherman Alexie**'s poetry and short-story collections include *The Business of Fancydancing* and *The Lone Ranger and Tonto Fistfight in Heaven*. After the publication of his first novel, *Reservation Blues*, Granta named him one of their Best Young American Novelists. His second novel, *Indian Killer*, was a *New York Times* notable book.

**Tom Andrews** received an M.F.A. in creative writing from the University of Virginia, Charlottesville, and later taught in the creative writing programs at Ohio University, Purdue University, and Warren Wilson University. A recipient of the 1999 Prix de Rome Fellowship in Literature from the American Academy of Arts and Letters and a Guggenheim Fellowship in 2001, his literary awards include an American Academy of Poets Prize and the Iowa Prize. He has published several acclaimed books of poetry, including *Hymning the Kanawha* (1989), *The Brother's Country* (1990), and *The Hemophiliac's Motorcycle* (1994), and a memoir, *Codeine Diary* (1998). Tom Andrews died in 2001.

**David Berman** was born in Williamsburg, Virginia, in 1967. He graduated from the Greenhill School in Addison, Texas; the University of Virginia; and the University of Massachusetts. His band, the Silver Jews, has released four albums, *The Natural Bridge*, *Starlite Walker*, *American Water*, and *Bright Flight*, on Drag City Records. He resides in Nashville, Tennessee.

**D. C. Berry**'s recent book is *Divorce Boxing*. He teaches at the University of Southern Mississippi.

**Paul Blackburn** was the author of nineteen books of poetry published between 1955 and 1980, the last six appearing posthumously. He translated the work of such writers as Pablo Picasso, Federico García Lorca, and Julio Cortázar. He died in 1971.

**Robert Bly** is an award-winning poet, translator, and editor. He started the influential literary magazine for poetry translation in the United States called, successively, *The Fifties*, *The Sixties*, and *The Seventies*, which he has recently revived as *The Thousands*. His most recent book of poems is *The Night Abraham Called to the Stars*, which won the Maurice English Award for poetry.

**Yves Bonnefoy,** French poet, essayist, translator, and art historian, is among the most widely translated and best-loved contemporary poets in France. In the United States he has held teaching positions at Brandeis University, Johns Hopkins University, Princeton University, Yale University, and the Graduate School, City University of New York.

**Marianne Boruch** has taught for a long time at Purdue University. Her four collections of poems include *View from the Gazebo* and *A Stick That Breaks and Breaks*, both published by Oberlin College Press, which will bring out her *New and Selected Poems* in 2004. Her book of personal essays on poetry, *Poetry's Old Air*, is published by the University of Michigan Press's "Poets on Poetry" series.

**Catherine Bowman** is the author of the poetry collections *Rock Farm* (1996) and *1-800-HOT-RIBS* (1993). Her writing has been awarded the Peregrine Smith Poetry Prize, the Kate Frost Discovery Award for Poetry, the Dobie Paisano Fellowship, a New York Foundation for the Arts Fellowship in Poetry, and two Yaddo Fellowships. In addition, Bowman reports on poetry for National Public Radio's *All Things Considered* and is the editor of *Word of Mouth* (Vintage Press, forthcoming). She teaches poetry at Indiana University.

*George Bradley* received a B.A. from Yale University (1975) and spent 1977–78 at the University of Virginia. *Terms to Be Met* won the Yale Younger Poet's Prize and was published by Yale University Press in 1985. Since 1982, Bradley has been a copywriter in New York City.

*Richard Brautigan* was born January 30, 1935, in the Pacific Northwest. In 1984, he committed suicide. He authored eleven books, nine books of poetry, and a collection of short stories. His daring imagination, humor, and haunting compassion continues to enthrall readers. Although Richard never learned to drive or owned a credit card, he loved the telephone.

*Dan Brown*, following studies in musical composition, turned to the computer field (and poetry). His poems have appeared in *Poetry*, *Partisan Review*, and other journals, and have been awarded a Pushcart Prize. His collection, *Matter* (Crosstown Books), is available from Amazon.com.

*Sharon Bryan* has won an Academy of American Poets Prize, the Discovery Award from *The Nation*, and two fellowships in poetry from the NEA. She is the author of the collections *Salt Air*, *Objects of Affection*, and *Flying Blind*, as well as editor of *Where We Stand: Women Poets on Literary Tradition*. She has been a visiting writer at many colleges and universities.

*Charles Bukowski* published his first story when he was twenty-four and began writing poetry at the age of thirty-five. His first book of poetry was published in 1959; he went on to publish more than forty-five books of poetry and prose, including *Pulp* (Black Sparrow, 1994), *Screams from the Balcony: Selected Letters 1960–1970* (1993), and *The Last Night of the Earth Poems* (1992). He died in 1994.

**Denver Butson** has published two books of poetry, *triptych* (The Commoner Press, 1999) and *Mechanical Birds* (St. Andrews College Press, 2000). His work has also appeared in anthologies such as *Ravishing Disunities* and *Ikons*, and in numerous journals, including *The Yale Review, Ontario Review, Caliban, Quarterly West*, and *Exquisite Corpse*.

**Karen Chase** lives, writes, and teaches in the Berkshire Mountains of Massachusetts. Her poems and stories have appeared in many magazines, including *The Gettysburg Review, The New Yorker, The New Republic*, and *The Yale Review*. Her book of poems, *Kazimierz Square*, came out in November 2000.

**Peter Cherches** is the author of two collections of short prose: *Condensed Book* (Benzene, 1986), and *Between a Dream and a Cup of Coffee* (Red Dust, 1987). His stories and prose poems have appeared in numerous magazines and anthologies, including *Harper's, Transatlantic Review, Fiction International, North American Review*, and *The Big Book of New American Humor*. Mr. Cherches lives in Brooklyn, New York, where he writes sparingly.

**Nicholas Christopher** is the author of seven books of poetry, most recently *Atomic Field: Two Poems*, and a book about film noir, *Somewhere in the Night*. His work has appeared in many magazines, including *The New Yorker, Esquire, The New Republic*, and *The Paris Review*. He has received numerous awards and fellowships from organizations, including the Guggenheim Foundation and the Academy of American Poets. He lives in New York City.

**Suzanne Cleary** is the author of *Keeping Time* (Carnegie Mellon, 2002). Her awards include the Cecil Hemley Memorial Award from the Poetry Society of America, and a fellowship from the New York Foundation for the Arts. She is associate professor of English at SUNY Rockland.

**David Clewell**'s most recent book of poetry is *Now We're Getting Somewhere* (University of Wisconsin Press, 1994), which won the Felix Pollack Prize in poetry.

**Lucille Clifton**'s most recent books of poetry include *Blessing the Boats: New and Selected Poems 1988–2000*, which won the National Book Award, and *The Terrible Stories* (1995), which was nominated for the National Book Award. She has served as Poet Laureate for the State of Maryland and is currently Distinguished Professor of Humanities at St. Mary's College of Maryland.

**Billy Collins**'s latest collection is *Nine Horses*. He is currently serving as Poet Laureate of the United States.

**Martha Collins** is the author of four collections of poems, the most recent of which is *Some Things Words Can Do* (Sheep Meadow, 1998). She has also co-translated *The Women Carry River Water*, a volume of poems by Vietnamese poet Nguyen Quang Thieu (UMass, 1997). She is Pauline Delaney Professor of Creative Writing at Oberlin College, where she also serves as editor of *FIELD* magazine.

**Geraldine Connolly**'s work has appeared in many magazines and journals, including *Poetry*, *Chelsea*, *The Gettysburg Review*, *The Georgia Review*, and *Shenandoah*. She lives with her family in Bethesda, Maryland, serves as executive editor of the literary quarterly *Poet Lore*, and teaches in the Johns Hopkins Graduate Writing Program in Washington, D.C.

**Peter Cooley,** a graduate of the Iowa Writer's Workshop, has taught creative writing at Tulane University in New Orleans since 1975. His seventh book, *A Place Made of Starlight,* has just been released by Carnegie Mellon University Press.

**Mary Cornish** completed her Master of Fine Arts degree in creative writing/poetry at Sarah Lawrence College. Her poems have appeared in *Poetry, New England Review, Alaska Quarterly, Rattapallax,* and *Poetry Northwest.* She is currently a Stegner Fellow in poetry at Stanford University.

**Jim Daniels**'s latest collection of poems, *Show and Tell: New and Selected Poems,* was published by the University of Wisconsin Press in 2003. His most recent collection of short fiction, *Detroit Tales,* was published by Michigan State University Press, also in 2003. He teaches at Carnegie Mellon University in Pittsburgh.

**Stephen Dobyns** has published eleven books of poetry, twenty novels, a book of short stories, and *Best Words, Best Order,* a book of essays on poetry. His most recent book of poetry is *The Porcupine's Kisses,* and his most recent work of fiction is *Eating Naked,* a volume of short stories. He lives in Boston and teaches at Sarah Lawrence College.

**Norman Dubie** has published more than twenty books of poetry. His most recent book is *Mercy Seat: Collected and New Poems,* published by Copper Canyon Press. He has just completed *The Spirit Tablets at Goa Lake,* a book-length poem in the science-fiction tradition that is appearing serially in *Blackbird.* He teaches at ASU and lives in Tempe, Arizona.

**Carol Ann Duffy** was born in Glasgow, Scotland, in 1955. She grew up in Stafford, England, and attended the University of Liverpool, where she received an honors degree in philosophy in 1977. Her poetry publications have received many awards, including both the Forward Prize and the Whitbread Prize for *Mean Time*. She has also written poems for children, including *Meeting Midnight*, recently published in England. Carol Ann Duffy is a Fellow of the Royal Society of Literature. She currently lives in Manchester, England, where she lectures on poetry for the Writing School at Manchester Metropolitan University.

**Stephen Dunn** is a Trustee Fellow in the Arts and professor of creative writing at Richard Stockton College in New Jersey. His book *Different Hours* was awarded the 2000 Pulitzer Prize for Poetry.

**Cornelius Eady** is the author of five books of poetry: *Kartunes* (1980); *Victims of the Latest Dance Craze* (1986); *The Gathering of My Name* (1991), nominated for the 1992 Pulitzer Prize in Poetry; *You Don't Miss Your Water* (1995); and *The Autobiography of a Jukebox* (1997). He has taught poetry at SUNY Stony Brook, where he directed its Poetry Center, and is presently Herbert Robinson Visiting Professor of Playwriting at The City College of New York. In January 2001 his sixth book of poetry, *Brutal Imagination*, was published by G. P. Putnam & Sons.

**Jenny Factor** is the winner of the 2000 Astraea Foundation grant in Poetry. Her first book, *Unraveling at the Name*, was published by Copper Canyon Press in 2003.

**B. H. Fairchild** is the author of *The Arrival of the Future*, *Local Knowledge*, *The Art of the Lathe*, and, most recently, *Early Occult Memory Systems of the Lower Midwest* (Norton, 2003), and has received fellowships from the Guggenheim and Rockefeller foundations and the National Endowment for the Arts.

**Edward Field** is a long-time resident of Greenwich Village, and with his partner, Neil Derrick, has written a novel, *The Villagers*.

During World War II, as navigator, he flew twenty-five bombing missions over Germany. Besides many honors for his poetry, the documentary *To Be Alive*, for which he wrote the narration, won an Academy Award.

**Donald Finkel** is the author of fifteen volumes of poetry, including his latest, *A Question of Seeing* (1998). His work has been published widely in literary magazines, and is represented in over sixty anthologies. Until 1991, he was Poet in Residence at Washington University.

**Nick Flynn** has worked at a variety of jobs, including ship's captain, electrician, and as a caseworker with homeless adults. *Some Ether*, a book of poems published by Graywolf Press, won a "Discovery"/The Nation Award as well as the PEN/American Center's Joyce Osterweil Award. He lives in Provincetown, Massachusetts, and in Brooklyn, New York.

**Aaron Fogel**'s *The Printer's Error* (Miami UP, 2001) is a collection of poems written between 1975 and 2000. Recent poems and essays have appeared in *Western Humanities Review*, *Matrix*, *Litrag*, *Pataphysics*, *Short Fuse*, and other journals. He teaches at Boston University.

**Chris Forhan** is the author of *Forgive Us Our Happiness*, which won the Bakeless Prize, and the forthcoming *The Actual Moon, The Actual Stars*, which won the Morse Prize. He teaches at Auburn University and in the Warren Wilson M.F.A. Program for Writers.

**Daisy Fried,** a 1989 graduate of Swarthmore College and contributor to numerous publications, including *Colorado Review*, *The New York Quarterly*, *The Antioch Review*, *The American Poetry Review*, and others, is a poet who has been informed by her ear as a journalist. She has worked as a staff writer at alternative weekly papers in Philadelphia and as a freelance contributor to regional publications, where she covered not only poetry but a wide range of social, political, and cultural issues.

*Dana Gioia* is a poet, critic, and literary anthologist. Author of the influential book *Can Poetry Matter?*, he is a long-time commentator for the BBC. His most recent volume of poetry, *Interrogations at Noon*, won the American Book Award.

*Jody Gladding*'s book, *Stone Crop*, appeared in the Yale Younger Poets Series in 1993. A chapbook, *Artichoke*, was published by Chapiteau Press in 2000. Gladding was a Stegner Fellow at Stanford, has taught at Cornell University, and won a Whiting Writers Award in 1997. She lives in East Calais, Vermont.

*Elton Glaser* edits the Akron Series in Poetry. He co-edited, with William Greenway, *I Have My Own Song for It: Modern Poems of Ohio* (University of Akron Press, 2002). His fifth full-length collection of poems, *Pelican Tracks*, winner of the Crab Orchard Award, appeared in 2003 from Southern Illinois University Press.

*Douglas Goetsch* is the author of four collections of poems, most recently, *First Time Reading Freud*, winner of the 2002 Permafrost competition. He lives in New York City, and teaches creative writing to incarcerated teens at Passages Academy in the Bronx.

*George Green* is a native of western Pennsylvania and long-time resident of New York City, where he earned an M.F.A. degree from The New School. His poems have recently appeared in *BOMB*, *Goodfoot*, and *Hanging Loose*.

*Eamon Grennan* is an Irish citizen who has lived in the United States for over thirty years. He is the Dexter M. Ferry Jr. Professor of English at Vassar College. His books include *Relations: New & Selected Poems* and *Still Life with Waterfall*, as well as a collection of translations—*Leopardi: Selected Poems*—and a volume of critical essays, *Facing the Music: Irish Poetry in the 20th Century.*

**Mark Halliday** teaches at Ohio University. His books of poems are *Little Star* (1987), *Tasker Street* (1992), *Selfwolf* (1999), and *Jab* (2002). He has also published a book on Wallace Stevens, and essays on poets Claire Bateman, Anne Carson, Carl Dennis, Kenneth Fearing, Allen Grossman, Kenneth Koch, Larry Levis, and others.

**Forrest Hamer** is the author of *Call & Response* (1995) and *Middle Ear* (2000). Born in North Carolina in 1956, he lives in the San Francisco Bay Area, where he works as a psychologist.

**Mac Hammond** was the author of *The Horse Opera, Cold Turkey, Six Dutch Hearts,* and *Mappamundi.* Born in Iowa and educated at Sewanee and Harvard, he lived in Buffalo and taught literature and creative writing at the State University until his death in 1997.

**Lola Haskins** has published seven books of poems, most recently *The Rim Benders* (Anhinga, 2001). BOA will publish *Desire Lines, New and Selected Poems* in 2004. Ms. Haskins's work has been broadcast on BBC and NPR, and has appeared in *The Atlantic Monthly, The Southern Review, The Georgia Review, Prairie Schooner, London Review of Books, London Magazine,* and elsewhere.

**Kaylin Haught** was born in Albion, Illinois, in 1947 and grew up on the Oklahoma prairie, where her father was an oil field worker and part-time preacher and her mother a housewife and part-time factory worker. She now lives in Seabrook, Texas, where she writes that "Poetry is my life, my joy, my work."

**Robert Hedin** is the author, translator, and editor of sixteen volumes of poetry and prose. Awards for his work include three

NEA Fellowships, and fellowships from the Bush Foundation, McKnight Foundation, and the Minnesota and North Carolina Arts Councils. He has taught at many universities throughout the country and is currently executive director of the Anderson Center, an artist community in Red Wing, Minnesota.

**Robert Hershon** is the author of eleven books of poetry, of which *The German Lunatic* is the most recent. Among his awards are two Creative Writing Fellowships from the National Endowment for the Arts and three from the New York Foundation of the Arts. Hershon is editor of Hanging Loose Press and executive director of The Print Center, Inc.

**Bob Hicok**'s most recent book, *Animal Soul*, was a finalist for the National Book Critics Circle Award. *Insomnia Diary* will be published by Pitt in 2004.

**David Hilton** was born in 1938 in Oakland, California. Since 1971, he has taught English at Anne Arundel Community College near Annapolis, Maryland. He has published his poems in such literary journals as *Poetry* and *The Yale Review*. His most recent book is *Smoke of My Own Breath* (Garlic Press, 2001).

**Edward Hirsch** is the author of *For the Sleepwalkers* (1981); *Wild Gratitude* (1986), which received the National Book Critics Circle Award; *The Night Parade* (1989); and *Earthly Measures* (1994). Hirsch has received a National Endowment for the Arts Fellowship, an Ingram Merrill Award, a Guggenheim Fellowship, and the Rome Prize from the American Academy and Institute of Arts and Letters. He teaches at the University of Houston.

**Tony Hoagland** has published two collections of poetry: *Sweet Ruin* (University of Wisconsin Press) and *Donkey Gospel* (Graywolf Press). His third collection, *What Narcissism Means to Me,* will appear in fall 2003. He currently teaches at the University of Pittsburgh and in the Warren Wilson M.F.A. program.

**John Hollander** has published seventeen books of poetry, including *Figurehead* and an expanded edition of his *Reflections on Espionage,* as well as seven books of criticism. Sterling Professor of English, Emeritus at Yale, he has received the Bollingen Prize and a MacArthur Fellowship, among others. *Picture Window,* his most recent book from Knopf, will appear in 2003.

**Elizabeth Holmes**'s first book of poetry, *The Patience of the Cloud Photographer,* was published in 1997 by Carnegie Mellon University Press. Her poems have appeared in such journals as *Poetry, Ploughshares, Michigan Quarterly Review, Southern Poetry Review, Prairie Schooner,* and *The Gettysburg Review.* A graduate of Davidson College and of the M.F.A. program in poetry at Cornell University, she works as a writer and editor in Ithaca, New York.

**Marie Howe** received a Guggenheim and a National Endowment for the Arts Fellowship. Her poems have appeared in *The New Yorker, The Atlantic Monthly, Agni, Harvard Review,* and *New England Review,* among others. She is the author of *The Good Thief,* which was selected by Margaret Atwood for the National Poetry Series. She teaches at Sarah Lawrence College.

**Andrew Hudgins** teaches at Ohio State University. His book, *Ecstatic in the Poison,* is due out from The Overlook Press in the summer of 2003. *Saints and Strangers* was a finalist for the Pulitzer Prize, *After the Lost War* received the Poets' Prize, and *The Never-Ending* was a finalist for the National Book Award.

**David Ignatow** has published fifteen volumes of poetry and three prose collections. Born in Brooklyn, he has lived most of his life in the New York metropolitan area, working as editor of *American Poetry Review* and *Beloit Poetry Journal*, and poetry editor of *The Nation*. He has received the Bollingen Prize, two Guggenheim fellowships, and countless other awards.

**Mark Irwin**'s fourth collection of poetry, *White City*, appeared from BOA in 2000. He is a visiting writer at the University of Colorado in Boulder. He lives in Denver and on a wilderness ranch in southern Colorado.

**Mark Jarman**'s latest collection of poetry is *Unholy Sonnets*. His previous collection, *Questions for Ecclesiastes*, won the Lenore Marshall Poetry Prize for 1998. He is the author of two books of essays on poetry: *The Secret of Poetry* and *Body and Soul: Essays on Poetry*. He teaches at Vanderbilt University.

**Lisa Jarnot** attended the State University of New York at Buffalo and Brown University. She has been the editor of two small poetry magazines, *No Trees* and *Troubled Surfer*, and is the author of *Ring of Fire* (Zoland).

**Louis Jenkins**'s books include *An Almost Human Gesture* (Eighties Press and Ally Press, 1987), *All Tangled Up With the Living* (Nineties Press, 1991), *Nice Fish: New and Selected Prose Poems* (Holy Cow! Press, 1995), *Just Above Water* (Holy Cow! Press, 1997), and *The Winter Road* (Holy Cow! Press, 2000).

**Kate Knapp Johnson** is the author of three collections of poetry, *When Orchids Were Flowers*, *This Perfect Life*, and *Wind Somewhere, And Shade* (Miami University Press Poetry Series), which received a 2001 Gradiva Award from the National Association for the Advancement of Psychoanalysis. She teaches at Sarah Lawrence College and is the director of their M.F.A. Program in Poetry. Johnson also has a private practice in psychoanalysis in Bedford Hills, New York.

**Richard Jones** is the author of several collections of poetry, including *The Blessing: New and Selected Poems* (Copper Canyon Press). His poems also appear in the recent anthologies *Good Poems*, *Poets of the New Century*, *Poetry in Motion*, and *The Poet's Child*.

**Katia Kapovich**'s poems have appeared in the *London Review of Books*, *Ploughshares*, *Harvard Review*, *The Antioch Review*, and *The American Scholar*, among others. A bilingual poet writing in English and Russian, she was the recipient of the 2001–2002 Witter Bynner Fellowship from the Library of Congress, and has published four collections of Russian poetry, as well as a novel in verse, *Suflior* (*The Prompter*). Katia currently resides in Cambridge, Massachusetts, where she is founder and editor (along with Philip Nikolayev) of an international English-language poetry magazine, *Fulcrum*.

**Jane Kenyon** was born in Ann Arbor and graduated from the University of Michigan. She is the author of four previous collections of poetry: *From Room to Room* (Alice James Books), *The Boat of Quiet Hours* (Graywolf Press), *Let Evening Come* (Graywolf Press), and *Constance* (Graywolf Press); and translator of *Twenty Poems of Anna Akhmatova* (Ally/The Eighties Press). Her poems have appeared in many magazines, including *The New Yorker*, *The Paris Review*, *The New Republic*, *The Atlantic Monthly*, and *Poetry*. She lived and worked with her husband, Donald Hall, in Wilmot, New Hampshire, until her death in 1995.

**Judith Kerman** was a Fulbright Senior Scholar in the Dominican Republic in 2002, translating poetry and fiction. Her most recent books are *Plane Surfaces/Plano de Incidencia* (CLDEH 2002, bilingual, translated by Johnny Durán) and *A Woman in Her Garden*, translations of Cuban poet Dulce María Loynaz (White Pine, 2002). She is professor of English at Saginaw Valley State University (Michigan).

*Galway Kinnell*'s books of poetry include *A New Selected Poems* (Houghton Mifflin, 2000), a finalist for the National Book Award; *Imperfect Thirst* (1996); *When One Has Lived a Long Time Alone* (1990); and *Selected Poems* (1980), for which he received both the Pulitzer Prize and the National Book Award. Galway Kinnell divides his time between Vermont and New York City, where he is the Erich Maria Remarque Professor of Creative Writing at New York University.

*David Kirby* is the W. Guy McKenzie Professor of English at Florida State University. A Johns Hopkins Ph.D., he is the recipient of five Florida State teaching awards. He is the author or co-author of twenty-one books. His work appears in the *Best American Poetry* and *Pushcart Prize* series, and a recent poetry collection, *The House of Blue Light*, was published in Louisiana State University Press's Southern Messenger series. LSU will also publish his next collection, *The Ha-Ha*.

*Bill Knott* was born in Carson City, Michigan.

*Kenneth Koch* has published more than twenty volumes of poetry; the most recent, *A Possible World* and *Sun Out: Selected Poems from 1952–1954*, were published posthumously in October 2002. His short plays, many of them produced off- and off-off-Broadway, are collected in *The Gold Standard: A Book of Plays* and *One Thousand Avant-Garde Plays*. He wrote several books about poetry, including *Wishes, Lies, and Dreams; Rose, Where Did You Get That Red?*; and *Making Your Own Days: The Pleasures of Reading and Writing Poetry*. He was a winner of the Bollingen Prize (1995), the Bobbitt Library of Congress Poetry Prize (1996), a finalist for the National Book Award (2000), and winner of the first annual Phi Beta Kappa Award for Poetry (2001). Kenneth Koch lived with his wife, Karen, in New York City and taught at Columbia University. He died in July 2002.

**Ronald Koertge** is the author of many books of poems; most recently, *Geography of the Forehead* (University of Arkansas Press). Besides awards for poetry like a NEA fellowship and being selected for inclusion in *The Best American Poetry 1999* anthology, he also writes fiction for young adults and teaches at Vermont College/Union Institute as part of the M.F.A. in Children's Writing program. A devoted handicapper, he has been known to drive many miles in wretched weather just to get a bet down.

**Ted Kooser** is a retired life insurance executive who lives on an acreage near the village of Garland, Nebraska. His poems have appeared in *The New Yorker, Hudson Review, The Antioch Review, The Kenyon Review, The Atlantic Monthly,* and dozens of other literary journals. He is the author of eight full-length collections of poetry, nine chapbooks and special editions, and a prose memoir.

**Steve Kowit** has been active for many years in antiwar and animal rights causes and is currently associated with organizations promoting Palestinian rights. He is the author of several collections of poetry, teaches at Southwestern College, and lives with his wife in the hills near the Mexican border.

**Dorianne Laux** is the author of three collections of poetry from BOA Editions: *Awake* (1990), introduced by Philip Levine; *What We Carry* (1994), finalist for the National Book Critics Circle Award; and *Smoke* (2000). She is also co-author, with Kim Addonizio, of *The Poet's Companion: A Guide to the Pleasures of Writing Poetry* (W.W. Norton, 1997).

**Naomi Lazard,** after studying graphic design at the Institute of Design in Chicago, began writing poetry in a workshop with John Logan at the University of Chicago. She has published six books of poetry, a book for children, short stories, and has written a stageplay, *The Elephant and the Dove,* a nonlinear drama whose subject is Frida Kahlo and the fate of art. She has received two National Endowment for the Arts Fellowships for poetry. She lives on the east end of Long Island with her snow dog, Muffin.

**David Lee** is the author of *The Porcine Legacy* (1974) and has been honored with grants from the National Endowment for the Arts and the National Endowment for the Humanities. Born in Matador, Texas, he currently lives in St. George and Pine Valley, Utah, with his wife, Jan, and children, Jon and JoDee.

**Li-Young Lee** was born in 1957 in Jakarta, Indonesia. He is the author of *Book of My Nights* (2001); *The City in Which I Love You* (1991); and *Rose* (1986), which won the Delmore Schwartz Memorial Poetry Award. He has also written a memoir entitled *The Winged Seed: A Remembrance* (1995), which received an American Book Award from the Before Columbus Foundation. He lives in Chicago with his wife, Donna, and their two sons.

**David Lehman** began writing a poem a day as an experiment in 1996. He is still at it. His books of poems include *The Daily Mirror* (2000) and *The Evening Sun* (2002). He has edited *Great American Prose Poems* and is series editor of *The Best American Poetry*.

**Jan Heller Levi** is the author of *Once I Gazed at You in Wonder* (1999), which won the 1998 Walt Whitman Award. She also edited *A Muriel Rukeyser Reader* (1994) and is currently working on *Rukeyser,* a biography. She has had recent residencies at Yaddo, the MacDowell Colony, and Ledig House International Colony. Jan Heller Levi divides her time between New York City and St. Gallen, Switzerland.

**Phillis Levin** is the author of the Norma Farber First Book Award winner *Temples and Fields,* and *The Afterimage.* Levin is also the recipient of an Amy Lowell Poetry Travelling Scholarship, an Ingram Merrill Grant, and a Fulbright Fellowship to Slovenia, and has been a fellow at the MacDowell Colony and Yaddo. Phillis Levin lives in New York City and teaches in the graduate program in creative writing at Hofstra University.

**Philip Levine** has received many awards for his books of poems, most recently the National Book Award in 1991 for *What Work Is*, and the Pulitzer Prize in 1995 for *The Simple Truth*.

**Larry Levis**'s books include *Wrecking Crew* (1972) and *The Afterlife* (1976). From 1992 until his death in 1996 at the age of forty-nine, he was a professor of English at Virginia Commonwealth University. His last collection, *Elegy* (edited by Philip Levine), was published posthumously in 1997.

**C. S. (Clive Staples) Lewis** (1898–1963) was the author of more than thirty books. His most distinguished and popular accomplishments include *The Chronicles of Narnia*, *Out of the Silent Planet*, *The Four Loves*, *The Screwtape Letters*, and *Mere Christianity*.

**Susan Ludvigson**'s seventh collection from Louisiana State University Press is *Sweet Confluence: New and Selected Poems* (2000). She has held Guggenheim, Rockefeller, Fulbright, and NEA fellowships and has represented the United States at literary festivals in France, Belgium, Canada, and Yugoslavia. She teaches at Winthrop University in Rock Hill, South Carolina.

**Alison Luterman**, raised in New England, moved to Oakland in 1990 where she has since worked as an HIV test counselor, a drug and alcohol counselor, a drama teacher, a poet in the schools, an actor in a children's theater troupe, and a freelance reporter. Her poems, feature articles, essays, and stories have appeared in *Kshanti*, *Slipstream*, *Poetry East*, *The Boston Phoenix*,

*The Boston Herald Sunday Magazine, The East Bay Express, Radiance, The Sun,* and *Whetstone.*

**Thomas Lux** holds the Bourne Chair in Poetry at Georgia Institute of Technology. His most recent book is *The Street of Clocks* (Houghton Mifflin, 2001).

**William Matthews** published eleven books of poetry during his lifetime, including *Time & Money* (1996), which won the National Book Critics Circle Award; *Selected Poems and Translations 1969–1991* (1992); *Blues If You Want* (1989); *A Happy Childhood* (1984); *Rising and Falling* (1979); *Sticks and Stones* (1975); and *Ruining the New Road* (1970). A twelfth collection was published posthumously as *After All: Last Poems* (1998). William Matthews died in 1997.

**Frances Mayes** is the author of *Under the Tuscan Sun,* an Italian memoir; *The Discovery of Poetry,* a text for readers; and five books of poetry, most recently *Ex Voto.* A frequent contributor to food and travel publications, she divides her time between Cortona, Italy, and San Francisco, where she is professor of creative writing at San Francisco State University. She is currently at work on a novel.

**Shara McCallum** is the author of two books of poems, both published by the University of Pittsburgh Press: *Song of Thieves* (2003) and *The Water Between Us* (1999), winner of the Agnes Lynch Starrett Prize for Poetry. Originally from Jamaica, she currently lives in Tennessee.

**Martha McFerren**'s poetry books include *Women in Cars* (1992) and *Contours for Ritual* (1988).

**Heather McHugh** regularly teaches in the low-residency M.F.A. program at Warren Wilson College in Asheville, North Carolina, as well as at the University of Washington at Seattle and the University of California at Berkeley. Her latest book of poems is entitled *Eyeshot*, to be published late in 2003 by Wesleyan University Press, which has also published her book of essays, *Broken English: Poetry and Partiality*.

**Lynne McMahon**'s new book, *Sentimental Standards*, will be out from David Godine in October 2003. Her previous books include *The House of Entertaining Science*, *Devolution of the Nude*, and *Faith*. She has received the Ingram-Merrill Award and a Guggenheim Foundation Grant. She lives in Columbia, Missouri, with her husband, Sherod Santos, and their two sons.

**Wesley McNair** has received fellowships from the Rockefeller, Fulbright, and Guggenheim Foundations, an NEH Fellowship in literature, and two NEA Fellowships for Creative Writers. Other honors include the Eunice Tietjens Prize from *Poetry*, the Theodore Roethke Prize from *Poetry Northwest*, and the Sarah Josepha Hale Medal. He has published several volumes, most recently a collection of poems, *Fire*, his fifth, and a book of essays, *Mapping the Heart*. Other poems appear at www.wesley mcnair.com.

**Peter Meinke** has published twelve books of poetry, including, most recently, *Scars* (1996) and *Zinc Fingers* (2000), both from the University of Pittsburgh Press. His poetry has received many prizes, and his collection of stories, *The Piano Tuner*, won the 1986 Flannery O'Connor Award. He lives in St. Petersburg, Florida.

**Samuel Menashe** was born in New York City in 1925. In 1943 he enlisted in the army and was sent to the Infantry School in Fort Benning, Georgia. After training in England, his division (the 87th) fought in France, Belgium (The Battle of the Bulge), and Germany. In 1950 he was awarded a *doctorat d'université* by the

Sorbonne. His first book, *The Many Named Beloved,* was published in London in 1961. In 1996, his poems were featured in *Penguin Modern Poets,* Volume 7, again published in London.

**Joseph Millar**'s poems have appeared in *DoubleTake, New Letters, Shenandoah, Ploughshares,* and *Manoa.* His first collection, *Overtime,* was published last year by Eastern Washington University Press, and he won a 2003 NEA fellowship. In 1997 he gave up his job as telephone installation foreman to try his hand at teaching.

**Susan Mitchell** is the author of three books of poems, most recently *Erotikon* (2000). Her previous collection, *Rapture,* won the Kingsley Tufts Poetry Award and was a National Book Award finalist. Mitchell grew up in New York City and now lives in Boca Raton, where she holds the Mary Blossom Lee Endowed Chair in Creative Writing at Florida Atlantic University.

**Elizabeth Seydel Morgan** is the author of four books of poetry, including *Parties* (1988), *The Governor of Desire* (1993), and *On Long Mountain* (1998). Morgan is a graduate of Hollins College and received her M.F.A. from Virginia Commonwealth University. She has also been the recipient of a grant from the National Endowment for the Humanities.

**Lisel Mueller**'s books of poetry include *Alive Together: New and Selected Poems* (1996), which won the Pulitzer Prize; *Learning to Play by Ear* (1990); *Waving from Shore* (1989); *Second Language* (1986); and *The Need to Hold Still* (1980), which received the National Book Award. Her honors include the Carl Sandburg Award and a National Endowment for the Arts Fellowship. She lives in Lake Forest, Illinois.

**Paul Muldoon** was born in Northern Ireland in 1951. He lives in New Jersey with his wife, the novelist Jean Hanff Korelitz, and their two children, and teaches at Princeton University. In 1999, he was elected Professor of Poetry at the University of Oxford.

**Taslima Nasrin** became a doctor in 1984 and her novel *Shame* brought her international feminist acclaim. She has published eighteen books in thirty different languages and has received many awards, including Feminist of the Year, USA (1994), the Human Rights Award from the Government of France, the International Humanist Award from the International Humanist and Ethical Union, and she has been named Global Leader for Tomorrow by the World Economic Forum.

**Edward Nobles** has published two books of poetry, *Through One Tear* and *The Bluestone Walk*. His poems have appeared in numerous magazines, including *The Gettysburg Review, The Kenyon Review, The Paris Review,* and *Tin House*. He lives in Bangor, Maine, where he is risk manager for the University of Maine System.

**Naomi Shihab Nye** lives in San Antonio, Texas. Her recent books include *19 Varieties of Gazelle: Poems of the Middle East*, a National Book Award finalist; *Habibi*, a novel for teens; and six anthologies of poetry for young readers. She recently received a Lannan Fellowship.

**Sharon Olds** was born in San Francisco and educated at Stanford and Columbia. Her books include *Satan Says; The Dead and the Living; The Gold Cell; The Wellspring; The Father; Blood, Tin, Straw;* and *The Unswept Room*. She was the New York State Poet Laureate from 1998 to 2000. She teaches poetry workshops in the Graduate Creative Writing Program at New York University and was one of the founders of the NYU workshop program at Goldwater Hospital on Roosevelt Island in New York. Her work has received the Harriet Monroe Prize, the National Book Critics Circle Award, the Lamont Selection of the Academy of American

Poets, the San Francisco Poetry Center Award, and a nomination for the National Book Award. She lives in New York City.

**Leanne O'Sullivan** is a first-year arts student at University College Cork, Ireland. She has been writing poetry since she was twelve, and has been published in Irish journals such as *The Stinging Fly*, *The Cork Literary Review*, *The Shop*, and *Poetry Ireland Review*, among others. She won the RTE Rattlebag poetry Slam (2002) and the Seacat Irish National Poetry Competition (Secondary School division 2001).

**Ron Padgett**'s books include *Oklahoma Tough: My Father, King of the Tulsa Bootleggers*, a memoir; *You Never Know*, poems; and *New & Selected Poems*. He is the editor of *The Teachers and Writers Handbook of Poetic Forms* and of *World Poets*, and the translator of Blaise Cendrars's *Complete Poems*.

**Elise Paschen** is the author of *Infidelities*, winner of the Nicholas Roerich Poetry Prize. She is the co-editor of *Poetry Speaks*; *Poetry in Motion*; and *Poetry in Motion from Coast to Coast*. Former executive director of the Poetry Society of America, Dr. Paschen teaches in the M.F.A. Writing Program at the School of the Art Institute of Chicago.

**Don Paterson** was born in Dundee in 1963. He works as a writer, editor, and musician, and teaches at the University of St. Andrews. He is the author of five collections of poetry. His literary awards include a Forward Prize, the T. S. Eliot Award, and the Geoffrey Faber Memorial Prize. A collection of his poetry, *The White Lie*, *New and Selected Poetry*, is published in the United States by Graywolf.

**G. E. Patterson** grew up in the middle of the country along the Mississippi River and was educated in the mid-South, the Midwest, the Northeast, and the western United States.

**Lucia Perillo**'s most recent book of poems is *The Oldest Map with the Name America* (Random House, 1999).

**Marc Petersen** writes, "My big cat follows me from room to room. She's black on top, with a white belly and paws, and a white tip on her tail. Her name's Penny. We found her at the pound. I love my wife too. We've been married twenty years. Poetry helps me clarify."

**Robert Phillips** is author of seven books of poetry and three collections of short stories. He teaches at the University of Houston. His prizes include an Award in Literature from the American Academy of Arts and Letters.

**Katha Pollitt** writes a column for *The Nation* about politics, culture, and feminism, and is the author of *Antarctic Traveller*, a collection of poems, and two collections of essays, *Reasonable Creatures* and *Subject to Debate*. She lives in New York City with her daughter, Sophie.

**Christina Pugh**'s chapbook *Gardening at Dusk* was published by Wells College Press in 2002. She has received *Poetry* magazine's Ruth Lilly Fellowship and the Grolier Poetry Prize. Her poems are published or forthcoming in *The Atlantic Monthly*, *Harvard Review*, *Columbia*, *Poetry Daily*, and other publications. She teaches at Northwestern University.

**Leroy V. Quintana**'s books include *Interrogations* (1990), *The History of Home* (1993), *My Hair Turning Grey Among Strangers* (1996), and *The Great Whirl of Exile: Poems* (1999), which solidified his place as a major force in Latino poetry. His work has won several awards, including the Before Columbus Foundation American Book Award (twice), as well as the El Paso Border Regional Library Association Award.

**David Ray**'s books include *Sam's Book*, *Wool Highways*, and *Demons in the Diner*. *The Endless Search*, a memoir, and *One Thousand Years*, Holocaust poems, are forthcoming. He has won many awards, gives readings and workshops, and can be reached at www.davidraypoet.com. Studs Terkel has written, "David Ray's poetry has always been radiant even though personal tragedy has suffused it."

**Alberto Ríos**'s most recent books include *Capirotada: A Nogales Memoir* (University of New Mexico Press, 1999); *The Curtain of Trees: Stories* (1999); and *Pig Cookies and Other Stories* (1995). He holds numerous awards, including the Arizona Governor's Arts Award and fellowships from the Guggenheim Foundation and the National Endowment for the Arts. Since 1994 he has been Regents Professor of English at Arizona State University, where he has taught since 1982. He lives in Chandler, Arizona.

**Yannis Ritsos,** born in 1909, was one of Greece's most prolific, distinguished, and celebrated poets whose many honors included the Alfred de Vigny Award (1975) and the Lenin Prize (1977). Ritsos died in 1990.

**Robin Robertson** is from the northeast coast of Scotland. *A Painted Field* won the 1997 Forward Prize for Best First Collection and the Scottish First Book of the Year Award. His second collection, *Slow Air*, has just been published by Harcourt.

**J. Allyn Rosser**'s first collection, *Bright Moves*, won the Morse Poetry Prize. *Misery Prefigured* appeared in 2001 from Southern Illinois University Press. Her work has received the Lavan Award for Younger Poets, the Frederick Bock Prize from *Poetry*, a Pushcart Prize, and fellowships from the National Endowment for the Arts and the Ohio Arts Council.

**Mary Ruefle** has published seven books of poetry, including *Among the Musk Ox People* (2002); *Post Meridian* (2000); *Cold Pluto* (1996); *The Adamant* (1989), winner of the 1988 Iowa Poetry Prize; *Life Without Speaking* (1987); and *Memling's Veil* (1982). She is the recipient of a 2002 Guggenheim Fellowship, an NEA Fellowship, a Whiting Writer's Award, and an Award in Literature from the American Academy of Arts and Letters.

**Timothy Russell,** despite working in a steel mill, somehow managed to win the 1993 Terrence Des Pres Prize in poetry from *Triquarterly* magazine for *Adversaria*, his first full-length book. He has published haiku in many journals.

**Mary Jo Salter** is the author of *A Kiss in Space* (2000); *Henry Purcell in Japan* (1985); *Unfinished Painting* (1989); and *Sunday Skaters* (1994); as well as a children's book, *The Moon Comes Home* (1989). An Emily Dickinson Lecturer in the Humanities at Mount Holyoke College, she lives in South Hadley, Massachusetts, with her husband, the writer Brad Leithauser, and their daughters, Emily and Hilary.

**Benjamin Saltman** has taught verse writing and contemporary American literature at California State University, Northridge, for twenty-five years, where he is Emeritus Professor of English.

**Ruth L. Schwartz** has published three books of poems: *Edgewater* (HarperCollins, 2002), selected by Jane Hirshfield as a 2001 National Poetry Series winner; *Singular Bodies* (Anhinga Press, 2001), winner of the 2000 Anhinga Prize for Poetry; and *Accordion Breathing and Dancing* (University of Pittsburgh Press, 1996), winner of the 1994 Associated Writing Programs competition.

**Evie Schockley**'s poetry appears in her chapbook *The Gorgon Goddess* (Carolina Wren Press, 2001) and in numerous journals, including *Beloit Poetry Journal, Brilliant Corners, Callaloo, Crab Orchard Review, nocturnes (re)view of the literary arts,* and *Obsidian III.* A graduate fellow of Cave Canem, Evie teaches literature at Wake Forest University.

**Shoshauna Shy**'s poems have recently appeared in *Cimarron Review, West Wind Review, The Comstock Review,* and *New Millennium Writings.* She is the author of two chapbooks produced by Pudding House Publications and Moon Journal Press. A member of the Wisconsin Fellowship of Poets, she works for the Wisconsin Humanities Council.

**Charles Simic** is one of America's leading poets, as well as an essayist and translator. His 1990 collection, *The World Doesn't End: Prose Poems,* was awarded the Pulitzer Prize, and he has received numerous other literary honors. Born in Belgrade, Simic now lives in New Hampshire, where he teaches American literature and creative writing at the University of New Hampshire.

**Hal Sirowitz**'s first collection, *Mother Said,* was published in 1996. He has been awarded a National Endowment for the Arts Fellowship. He has appeared on MTV's *Spoken Word Unplugged* and at the Lollapalooza Festival. And he has been featured on PBS's *The United States of Poetry* and on NPR's *All Things Considered.* He lives in Flushing, New York.

**Carol Snow** is the author of *Artist and Model,* winner of the 1990 Book Award from the Poetry Center at San Francisco State University. She is the recipient of a National Endowment for the Arts Fellowship and lives in San Francisco.

**Gary Soto** is the author of twenty-five books for children, young adults, and adults, including *Living Up the Street, Buried Onions,* and *Baseball in April.* He serves as Young People's Ambassador for California Rural Legal Assistance (CRLA) and the United Farm Workers of America (UFW). He lives in Berkeley, California.

**Gerald Stern**'s most recent books of poetry include *Last Blue: Poems* (2000); *This Time: New and Selected Poems* (1998), which won the National Book Award; *Odd Mercy* (1995); and *Bread Without Sugar* (1992). His honors include the Ruth Lilly Prize, four National Endowment for the Arts grants, and fellowships from the Academy of American Poets, the Guggenheim Foundation, and the Pennsylvania Council on the Arts. For many years a teacher at the University of Iowa Writers' Workshop, he lives in Easton, Pennsylvania, and New York City.

**Henry Taylor**'s five collections of poems include *The Flying Change*, winner of the 1986 Pulitzer Prize in Poetry, and *Brief Candles: 101 Clerihews.* He is professor of literature at American University in Washington, D.C.

**John Updike** is the author of more than fifty books, including collections of short stories, poems, essays, and criticism. His novels have won the Pulitzer Prize (twice), the National Book Award, the National Book Critics Circle Award, the Rosenthal Award, and the Howells Medal.

**Luisa Villani** is a world traveler. Her first book, *Running Away from Russia*, won the Bordighera Prize and was published by Purdue University. She has received a Pennsylvania Council on the Arts Grant, and is working on a second book of poetry about Chiapas, Mexico.

**Diane Wakoski**, who was born and raised in Southern California, has published more than twenty collections of poetry, the most recent of which is *The Butcher's Apron* (Black Sparrow

Press), new and selected poems on the theme of eating and drinking. She is Poet in Residence at Michigan State University.

**Ronald Wallace** is the author of twelve books of poetry, fiction, and criticism, including *The Makings of Happiness* (1991), *Time's Fancy* (1994), *The Uses of Adversity* (1998), and *Long for This World: New and Selected Poems* (2003), all from the University of Pittsburgh Press. He co-directs the creative writing program at the University of Wisconsin at Madison.

**Connie Wanek** is the author of two books of poems, *Bonfire* (New Rivers Press, 1997) and *Hartley Field* (Holy Cow! Press, 2002). She grew up in Wisconsin and New Mexico, and currently lives in Duluth, Minnesota.

**Tom Wayman** has published thirteen collections of his poems, most recently *Did I Miss Anything? Selected Poems 1973–93* (1993) and *The Astonishing Weight of the Dead* (1994).

**Charles Webb**'s book *Reading the Water* (Northeastern University Press) won the 1997 Morse Poetry Prize and the 1998 Kate Tufts Discovery Award. He recently received a 1998 Whiting Writer's Award.

**Rebecca Wee**'s first book of poetry, *Uncertain Grace*, won the 2000 Hayden Carruth Award for New and Emerging Poets. She is also a recipient of a 2003–04 Witter Bynner Fellowship from the Library of Congress to support the writing of poetry. She teaches at Augustana College in Rock Island, Illinois.

**Bruce Weigl** is the author of twelve collections of poetry, most recently *Archeology of the Circle: New and Selected Poems* (1999) and *After the Others* (1999). Weigl has been awarded a Patterson Poetry Prize, the Pushcart Prize (twice), an award from the

Academy of American Poets, a Yaddo Foundation Fellowship, and a National Endowment of the Arts grant.

**Joe Wenderoth** grew up near Baltimore. Wesleyan University Press published his first two books of poems, *Disfortune* (1995) and *It Is If I Speak* (2000). Shortline Editions published a chapbook, *The Endearment* (1999), and Verse Press published a novel, *Letters to Wendy's*, in 2000. Wenderoth is assistant professor of English at Southwest State University in Marshall, Minnesota.

**Reed Whittemore**'s first poetry book, *Heroes and Heroines*, was published in 1947, fresh from his experience in the U.S. Air Force. Since then he has published fifteen books of poetry and prose. A teacher at Carleton College and emeritus professor of English at University of Maryland, Whittemore served twice as Poetry Consultant for the Library of Congress. He currently lives in College Park, Maryland.

**Nancy Willard** is the author of many poems, novels, and award-winning children's books, including *A Visit to William Blake's Inn*. She is a lecturer at Vassar College and lives with her husband in Poughkeepsie, New York.

**Miller Williams**, University Professor of English and Foreign Languages at the University of Arkansas, is author, editor, or translator of thirty books, including twelve collections of poetry. He has received the Academy Award for Literature and the Prix de Rome from the American Academy of Arts and Letters, as well as the Poets' Prize and a New York Arts Fund Award for Distinguished Contribution to American Letters, among other awards.

**Robley Wilson** edited *The North American Review* for more than thirty years. Since his retirement he has lived in Florida with his wife, Susan Hubbard, and numerous cats. His most recent poetry collection is *Everything Paid For*. His second novel, *Splendid Omens*, is forthcoming from St. Martin's.

**Terence Winch**'s work has appeared in many publications, among them *The Paris Review*, *New American Writing*, *The New Republic*, and *The American Poetry Review*, and in many anthologies, including *Best American Poetry*. The subject of a profile on NPR's *All Things Considered*, Winch has also been the recipient of a National Endowment for the Arts Fellowship and other grants. His books have won an American Book Award and the Columbia Book Award. His most recent book is *The Drift of Things* (The Figures, 2001).

**David Wojahn** is the author of seven collections of poetry, including *Spirit Cabinet* (2002) and *Strange Good Fortune: Essays on Contemporary Poetry* (2001). He is the recipient of a National Endowment for the Arts Creative Writing Fellowship, the Amy Lowell Traveling Poetry Scholarship, the William Carlos Williams Book Award, and the George Kent Memorial Prize from *Poetry*.

**Robert Wrigley** teaches in the creative writing program at the University of Idaho. A former Guggenheim and two-time NEA Fellow, he has published five books of poetry, including *Reign of Snakes*, winner of the 2000 Kingsley Tufts Award. His lives in the woods near Moscow, Idaho, with his wife, the writer Kim Barnes, and their children.

**Mark Wunderlich** is the author of *The Anchorage*, which received the 1999 Lambda Literary Award for poetry. Twice a Fellow at the Work Center, he has taught at Barnard College, Stanford University, and in the Graduate Writing Program of both San Francisco State University and Ohio University.

**Jane Yolen** writes children's books, fantasy, science fiction, poetry, book reviews, and nonfiction. She has won numerous awards, including the Caldecott Medal, two Nebula Awards, the

World Fantasy Award, three Mythopoeic Fantasy Awards, the Golden Kite Award, the Jewish Book Award, and the Association of Jewish Libraries Award. She and her husband divide their time between a one-hundred-year-old farmhouse in Hatfield, Massachusetts, and a house called "Wayside" in Scotland.

**David Young** is the author of nine books of poetry, most recently, *At the White Window*. He is also the author of *Seasoning: A Poet's Year*, and of a forthcoming translation of the poems of Petrarch.

**Dean Young** is the author of four books of poems: *First Course in Turbulence* (University of Pittsburgh, 1999); *Strike Anywhere* (1995); *Design with X* (1988); and *Beloved Infidel* (1992). Currently an associate professor of English and creative writing at Loyola University, he splits his time between Chicago and Berkeley, California, where he lives with his wife, fiction writer Cornelia Nixon.

**Kevin Young**'s poetry books include *Most Way Home, To Repel Ghosts*, and, most recently, *Jelly Roll*. A former Stegner Fellow in Poetry at Stanford University, Young is currently Ruth Lilly Professor of Poetry at Indiana University.

**Adam Zagajewski** was born in Lvov in 1945. His books include the poetry collections *Tremor* (1985), *Canvas* (1992), and *Mysticism for Beginners* (1998), and the essay collections *Two Cities* (1995) and *Another Beauty* (2000). He lives in Paris and Houston (where he teaches at the University of Houston).

**Paul Zimmer** has published eight books of poetry, including *Family Reunion*, which won an Award for Literature from the Academy and Institute of Arts and Letters; *The Great Bird of Love*; *Big Blue Train*; and *Crossing to Sunlight: Selected Poems*. A book of memoirs and essays, *After the Fire: A Writer Finds His Place*, was just published by the University of Minnesota Press.

# *index of contributors*

# index of titles

# permission credits

Grateful acknowledgment is made to the following for
permission to reprint previously published material:

*Alice James Books:* "Old Men Playing Basketball" from *the Art of the Lathe* by
B. H. Fairchild, copyright © 1998 by B. H. Fairchild. "Lesson" from *Call &
Response* by Forrest Hamer. Copyright © 1995 by Forrest Hamer. All poetry
reprinted by permission of Alice James Books.

*Literary Estate of Tom Andrews:* "Six One-Line Film Scripts" by Tom Andrews,
originally published in *Hotel Amerika,* Vol. 1, No. 1, Fall, 2002, copyright © 2002
by the Literary Estate of Tom Andrews. Reprinted by permission of the Literary
Estate of Tom Andrews.

*D. C. Berry:* "Hamlet Off-Stage: Laertes Cool" by D. C. Berry, originally
published in *Tar River Poetry,* Vol. 39, No. 2, Spring 2000. Copyright © 2000 by
D. C. Berry. Reprinted by permission of the author.

*BOA Editions, Ltd.:* "praise song" from *Blessing the Boats: New and Selected Poems
1988–2000* by Lucille Clifton, copyright © 2000 by Lucille Clifton. "Advice from
the Experts" from *Laugh at the End of the World: Collected Comic Poems 1969–1999*
by Bill Knott, copyright © 2000 by Bill Knott; "Alzheimer's" from *Plus Shipping*
by Bob Hicok, copyright © 1998 by Bob Hicok; "A Myopic Child" from *Selected
Poems 1939–1988,* by Yannis Ritsos, edited and translated by Kimon Friar and
Kostas Myrsiades with additional translations by Athan Anagnostopoulos,
copyright © 1988 by BOA Editions, Ltd.; "Singing Back the World" from *What
We Carry* by Dorianne Laux, copyright © 1994; "Little Father" and "Words for
Worry" from *Book of My Nights* by Li-Young Lee, copyright © 2001 by Li-Young
Lee. All poetry reprinted by permission of The Permissions Company, Rights
Agency for BOA Editions, Ltd.

*Catherine Bowman:* "1-800-HOT-RIBS" from *1-800-Hot-Ribs* by Catherine
Bowman (Gibbs Smith, 1993), copyright © 1993 by Catherine Bowman.
Reprinted by permission of the author.

*George Braziller, Inc.:* "The Partial Explanation" and "Bestiary for the Fingers of
My Right Hand" from *Charles Simic: Selected Early Poems* by Charles Simic,

*Wesley McNair:* "Goodbye to the Old Life" by Wesley McNair, originally published in *Poetry Northwest*, Volume XLII, No. 1, Spring, 2001. Copyright © 2001 by Wesley McNair. Reprinted by permission of the author.

*Wesley McNair and David R. Godine, Publisher, Inc.:* "Killing the Animals" from *The Town of No* by Wesley McNair. Copyright © 1998 by Wesley McNair. Reprinted by permission of the author and David R. Godine, Publisher, Inc.

*Samuel Menashe:* "49th Birthday Trip" from *The Niche Narrows* (Talisman House, 2000) by Samuel Menashe. Reprinted by permission of the author.

*Miami University Press:* "The Meadow" from *Wind Somewhere, and Shade* by Kate Knapp Johnson, copyright © 2001 by Kate Knapp Johnson. "The Printer's Error" from *The Printer's Error* by Aaron Fogel, copyright © 2001 by Aaron Fogel. All poetry reprinted by permission of Miami University Press.

*New Letters:* "My Father's Hats" by Mark Irwin, originally published in *New Letters*, Vol. 66, No. 3, Spring 2000, reprinted here with the permission of *New Letters* and the Curators of the University of Missouri-Kansas City.

*Northeastern University Press:* "Message: Bottle #32" from *Bright Moves* by J. Allyn Rosser, copyright © 1990 by J. Allyn Rosser. "The Death of Santa Claus" from *Reading the Water* by Charles Harper Webb, copyright © 1997 by Charles Harper Webb. All poetry reprinted by permission of Northeastern University Press.

*Northwestern University Press:* "In Simili Materia" from *Adversaria* by Timothy Russell (Evanston, IL: Northwestern University Press, 1993, p. 27), copyright © 1993 by Timothy Russell. "May" from *What Saves Us* by Bruce Weigl (Evanston, IL: Northwestern University Press, 1994, p. 57), copyright © 1992 by Bruce Weigl. First published in 1992 by TriQuarterly Books. Northwestern University Press/TriQuarterly Books edition published 1994. All rights reserved. Reprinted by permission of Northwestern University Press.

*Naomi Shihab Nye:* "For Mohammad Zeid, Age 15" and "Rain" both by Naomi Shihab Nye. Reprinted by permission of the author.

*Oberlin College Press:* "The Book of Hand Shadows" by Marianne Boruch from *A Stick That Breaks and Breaks*, the FIELD Poetry Series, v. 5, Oberlin, OH, Oberlin College Press, 1997. Reprinted by permission of Oberlin College Press.

*Ohio State University Press:* "Poem for Adlai Stevenson and Yellow Jackets" by David Young, originally published in *At the White Window* (2000). Reprinted by permission of Ohio State University Press.

*Sharon Olds:* "The Space Heater" by Sharon Olds, originally published in *The New Yorker*, January 22, 2001. Reprinted by permission of the author.

*Open City Books:* "Snow" from *Actual Air* by David Berman. Copyright © 1999 by David Berman. Reprinted by permission of Open City books.